Thomas Carlyle, Charles Eliot Norton

Early Letters

Edited by Charles Eliot Norton. Vol. I (1814 - 1821)

Mr. Froude, however, thought otherwise, and has given to the public an "express biography" of him. The view of Mr. Carlyle's character presented in this biography has not approved itself to many of those who knew Carlyle best. It may be a striking picture, but it is not a good portrait.

For the present, at least, it appears impracticable to prepare another formal biography. The peculiar style of Mr. Froude's performance, already in possession of the field, might perhaps put a portrait of Carlyle drawn by a hand more faithful to nature, and less skilled in fine artifices than his own, at a temporary disadvantage with the bulk of readers. But it has seemed right to print some of Carlyle's letters in suchwise that with his *Reminiscences* they might serve as a partial autobiography, and illustrate his character by unquestionable evidence. They do not indeed afford a complete portrait; but so far as they go the lines will be correct.

The earliest letters of Carlyle that are
known to exist are those which he wrote in
1814 and the three or four following years,
while he was at Annan, Edinburgh, and Kirkcaldy. He seldom let a week pass without
sending a letter home; not infrequently he
wrote three or even four to different members
of his family on the same day. I have printed
a large number of these letters in spite of the
sameness in their tone and topics, because of
the light they throw upon Carlyle's character
during an important period in his intellectual
growth, and also because they are of more
than personal interest from the striking illus-
tration they afford of the simpler side of
Scottish life.

Carlyle's chief correspondents, outside his
own family, during the first years after his
leaving the University, were three college
friends, James Johnstone, Robert Mitchell, and
Thomas Murray.

Carlyle, in his later years, writing of John-

stone, says, "He was six or seven years my
elder, but very fond of discoursing with me,
and much my companion while we were in
Annandale together within reach.   A poor and
not a very gifted man, but a faithful, diligent,
and accurate; of quietly pious, candid, pure
character,—and very much attached to me.
In return I liked him honestly well; learnt
something from him (the always diligently
exact in book-matters); perhaps ultimately
taught him something; and had great satisfaction in his company (in the years 1814-16, and
occasionally afterwards)."   Mainly through the
efforts of Miss Welsh (made for Carlyle's sake),
he was in 1826 appointed Parish Schoolmaster
at Haddington, where, towards the end of
1837, he died.

Mitchell was an Annandale man, who upon
leaving college had looked forward to becoming
a minister in the Scotch Kirk; but, like Carlyle,
he soon gave up this outlook, and he became
and remained a schoolmaster.   He was for

some years tutor in the family of the Rev. Henry Duncan, of Ruthwell, Dumfriesshire, was afterwards Rector of the Grammar School at Kirkcudbright, and latterly one of the masters of the Edinburgh Academy. Carlyle notes in his journal, 1st August 1836 : " Poor R. Mitchell dead, and buried with public funeral, Calton Hill, Edinburgh ; many sad thoughts I had sent towards him, but in silence."

Thomas Murray was a cheery, kindly youth. He became a minister, wrote a respectable literary history of Galloway, his native county, was for a time editor of the *Edinburgh Weekly Chronicle*, and lived to a good old age.

Still more interesting than these letters would have been Carlyle's letters to Edward Irving, but it is believed that they were destroyed after Irving's death.

As to what use I might be justified in making of another series of letters at my disposal, those from Carlyle to Miss Welsh from their

first acquaintance in 1821 until their marriage
in 1826, I have felt grave doubts. The letters
of lovers are sacred confidences, whose sanctity
none ought to violate. Mr. Froude's use of
these letters seems to me, on general grounds,
unjustifiable, and the motives he alleges for it
inadequate. But Carlyle himself had strictly
forbidden their printing. When he was edit-
ing the *Letters and Memorials of Jane Welsh
Carlyle*, of her letters to him, and of his to her
which were written before their marriage, only
one short note from Miss Welsh, dated 3d September 1825, printed by Mr. Froude (*Life*,[1] i.
308, 309), could be found; the rest were missing.
To the copy of this short note Carlyle appends
the words, " In pencil all but the address.
Original strangely saved ; and found accident-
ally in one of the presses to-day. HER note,
when put down by the coach, on that visit to
us at Hoddam Hill in September 1825! How—

─────────

[1] *Thomas Carlyle : A History of the First Forty Years of
his Life*, by J. A. Froude. London, 1882.

mournful now, how beautiful and strange! A relic to me priceless (T. C., 12th March 1868)." As to the then missing Letters written before their marriage, his and Miss Welsh's, Carlyle, in the original manuscript from which the copy given to Mr. Froude was made, says, " My strict command now is, ' Burn them, if ever found. Let no third party read them ; let no *printing* of them, or of any part of them, be ever thought of by those who love me !' "

I decided not to open the parcels containing these letters. But I was gradually led by many facts to the conviction that Mr. Froude had distorted their significance, and had given a view of the relations between Carlyle and his future wife, in essential respects incorrect and injurious to their memory. I therefore felt obliged to read these letters, which I have done with extreme reluctance, and with reverential respect for the sacredness of their contents. The conviction which determined me to read them was confirmed by the perusal.

The question then arose whether further publication of them was justifiable for the sake of correcting the view presented by Mr. Froude. The answer seemed plain, that only such of these letters, or such portions of them, as had not any specifically private character could rightly be printed. I have therefore printed comparatively few of Carlyle's letters to Miss Welsh, while, in an Appendix to Volume II., I have tried to set right some of the facts misrepresented by Mr. Froude, and to show his method of dealing with his materials.

CHARLES ELIOT NORTON.

CAMBRIDGE, MASSACHUSETTS,
July 1886.

MEMBERS OF CARLYLE'S FAMILY.

JAMES CARLYLE (born at Brownknowe, near Ecclefechan, August 1758; died at Scotsbrig, 22d January 1832) married, 5th March 1795, MARGARET AITKEN (born at Whitestanes, Kirkmahoe, Dumfriesshire, 30th September 1771 ; died at Scotsbrig, 25th December 1853.

The following is a List of their Children :—

THOMAS, born 4th December 1795; died at Chelsea 5th February 1881.

ALEXANDER, born 4th August 1797 ; died in Canada 30th March 1876.

JANET, born 2d September 1799 ; died 8th February 1801.

JOHN AITKEN, born 7th July 1801 ; died at Dumfries 15th September 1879.

MARGARET, born 20th September 1803 ; died 22d June 1830..

JAMES, born 12th November 1805. ⎫
MARY, born 2d February 1808. ⎪ These still survive
JANE, born 2d September 1810. ⎬ (July 1886).
JANET, born 18th July 1813. ⎭

LETTERS

OF

THOMAS CARLYLE

I.—To Mr. THOMAS CARLYLE, Edinburgh.

From his FATHER.[1]

ECCLEFECHAN, *27th April* 1814.

DEAR SIR—I received yours yesterday, and was very glad to hear that you were well and was teaching, for we did not know what to do, whether you were coming home or going to stop at Edinburgh; the reason of me not writing last time the Carrier came out—Sandy[2]

[1] This letter is apparently the earliest that has been preserved of the long correspondence between Carlyle and his family. [My Father] "wrote to me duly and affectionately while I was at college. Nothing that was good for me did he fail with his best ability to provide."—*Reminiscences*, i. 58.

[2] Carlyle's next younger brother. What "Dr. Thom's Mob"

was summoned about Dr. Thom's Mob; he was libled with thirteen pages of paper written about the business. Dr. Henderson and Tom Minto were likewise summoned, and Peggy Kerr; there being no proof against Sandy he of course was discharged from the Bar. Dr. Henderson was fined £20 and one month's imprisonment; Minto, £10 and two week's imprisonment; Peggy Kerr, £5. We were all in confusion on Saturday getting witnesses to prove Sandy not guilty, and after all our labour the witnesses would not do without your Mother was there also; then she had to get ready for setting off on Monday, which she did with great difficulty, having to take Jenny and Peggy with her. You may think whether that would put us past writing or not. The Carrier is for coming off on Monday; but I thought that would not do for you [which] caused me to write this in the meantime and enclose this, and I will send your things with the Carrier. In the meantime I think these two guineas will

was and what share, if any, the boy Sandy had in it, there is now no telling.

clear you. As I am in haste I will add no
more at present. Mention in your next if you
got the Single Note with the Box, etc.

JAS. CARLYLE.

II.—To Mr. ROBERT MITCHELL, Linlithgow.

EDINBURGH, 30th April 1814.

DEAR MITCHELL—You are perhaps thinking
by this time that I am slow in answering your
long-solicited letter; and before going further, I
must beg pardon, and plead the trite excuses of
business, indolence, etc. etc.—and let me tell
you, you have been such a notorious offender
in that way yourself, you can't have the im-
pudence to make any complaints.

Were I disposed to moralise, there is before
me the finest field that ever opened to the eye
of mortal man. *Nap the mighty*, who, but a
few months ago, made the sovereigns of Europe
tremble at his nod; who has trampled on
thrones and sceptres, and kings and priests,
and principalities and powers, and carried ruin
and havoc and blood and fire, from Gibraltar

to Archangel—*Nap the mighty* is—GONE TO POT!!!

"I will plant my eagles on the towers of Lisbon. I will conquer Europe and crush Great Britain to the centre of the terraqueous globe." I will go to Elba *and be coop'd up* in Limbo!!! But yesterday, and *Boney* might have stood— against the world ; now " none so poor to do him rev'rence." " Strange," says Sancho Panza, "very strange things happen in the boiling of an egg." All those fine things, however, and twenty thousand others have been thought and said by everybody who thinks or speaks upon the subject—and so I leave them.

Having got out of this rhapsody, I now proceed to consider the contents of your letter. It gives me the sincerest sorrow, that you *did not* accomplish that redoubtable undertaking in which you were engaged.[1] There is a real

---

[1] Mitchell, in his letter (from Linlithgow, 9th April) to which this is an answer, had written as follows. The passage is characteristic, and shows his liveliness of spirit and his studious bent: "For three or four days I was idle ; but idleness is the inlet to every mischief. The wildest notion that ever entered into mortal man's brain took such possession of

pleasure attends those same castles which all of us so often build, and though, "like the baseless fabric of a vision," they must "all dissolve and leave not a rack behind," still there is enjoyment while the illusion lasts. The trisection of an angle by simple geometry is a complete *wild-goose chase*, at any rate, and in it disappointments must be *relied on*. Still your achievement (even had it come that length) was but like the drop in the bucket to some of *my projected* exploits. 'Twas but the other day, for instance, that I had got into a sure and expeditious way of boring a hole, right, slap, souse down through the centre of the earth we

my poor cranium that I believe it was as effectually deranged by Leslie's *Geometry* as ever the valiant Knight of La Mancha's by Amadis de Gaul. In short, I believed it was destined for me to solve the problem of the trisection of an angle. I'll not tell you how many solar revolutions were performed whilst I was possessed with this Mathematical frenzy. Need I tell you how long after midnight I watched my armour of scale and compasses,—how often I believed that I had wrought the doughty deed, and secured to myself the applause of a wondering world? Truly I might be denominated the Knight of the Rueful Countenance, when I returned to curse the hour in which I undertook the desperate enterprise. I am now content to read Sharp's *Sermons*, the *Border Minstrel*, and even the *Confession of Faith!*"

inhabit, and receiving point blank the productions of New Zealand and the South Sea !!!!

As I will be in Edinburgh at least *part* of the summer, I cannot but highly approve of the plan you proposed of sending our essays to be remarked on by each other. It is impossible that it *could* do any *harm :* and since it would afford a very useful exercise *at least*, it would, I am convinced, be a very profitable way of carrying on our correspondence. I shall expect, therefore, in a few days to receive, per Carrier, a paper of yours to peruse, and directions how to proceed, with regard to time, etc. etc. Don't be particular as to the choice of a subject—*any* will do. It is very likely that I may send you some Mathematical thing or other, seeing I have got Bossut's *History of Mathematics* at this time, where perhaps there may be something new to you ;—and again, I stumbled the other night upon a kind of a new demonstration of Pythagoras' *square of the hypotenuse ;* and if you don't find it yourself (most likely you will), I will send you it too. We need be at no loss for subjects, literary, metaphysical, mathematical, and physical are all before us. I am sure this would be a very good way of spending part of the summer; and you who are the *projector* will surely never draw back from what you yourself proposed, and therefore *will not fail* to send me your production the very next opportunity.

Firmly had I resolved, on the faith of your recommendation, to read *Thaddeus*,[1] and you may believe me, when I declare that it was not for want of exertion on my part that I have not seen it yet. The truth is, I am acquainted only in one circulating library, and there *Thaddeus* has always been "out." Getting a book from a strange library is a little troublesome, and thus expecting every day to get it from that where I am known, I made no effort elsewhere. However, I *will* have it read, *if possible*, before I address you again—which, if you stick to promises, will not be long.

By the way, you have heard of Dr. John

[1] Miss Jane Porter's high-flown romance of *Thaddeus of Warsaw*, published in 1803, but still, in 1814, much admired by young people.

Leyden,[1] the unfortunate author of *Scenes of Infancy*, etc., from (I believe) Roxburghshire, who went to India and met an untimely end.

> Leyden, a shepherd wails thy fate,
> And Scotland knows her loss too late.—HOGG.

Well, if I am not much deceived, you will thank me for transcribing the following poem of his, composed on (Wellington, then) Wellesley's victory at Assaye, while Leyden was in India. I met with it in *The Spy*, a kind of periodical thing published the other year in Edinburgh.

> Shout, Britons, for the battle of Assaye;
>   . For that was a day,
>   When we stood in our array,
>   Like the Lion's might at bay;
> And our battle-word was Conquer or Die.

> Rouse, rouse the cruel leopard from his lair,
>   With his yell the mountain rings;
>   And his red eye round he flings,
>   As arrow-like he springs,
> And spreads his clutching paw to rend and tear.

---

[1] Leyden died in 1811; his memory is kept alive by Scott's sympathetic biography of him—one of those biographical sketches which give a high impression alike of its subject and its author.

Then first array'd in battle front we saw,
    Far as the eye could glance,
    The Mahratta banners dance,
    O'er the desolate expanse,
And their standard was the leopard of Malwa.

But when we first encountered man to man,
    Such odds came never on
    Against Greece at Marathon
    When they shook the Persian throne,
'Mid the old barbaric pomp of Ispahan.

No number'd might of living men could tame
    Our gallant band that broke
    Through the bursting clouds of smoke,
    When the vollied thunder spoke,
From a thousand mouldering mouths of lurid flame.

.   .   .   .   .

Shout, Britons, for the battle of Assaye;
    Ye who perished in your prime,
    Your hallowed names sublime,
    Shall live to ceaseless time,
Your heroic worth and fame shall never die.

Can anything be grander? what *fire!* what *energy!* If there is anything in existence that surpasses this, it must be Hohenlinden—but what is like Hohenlinden? Tell me in your next what you think of this piece. Is not, think you, "From a thousand *mouldering* mouths of lurid flame" misprinted somehow? Would "smouldering" do any better? . . . .

Do not neglect to write to me *immediately*, and send me your essay—no matter what about. Tell me too, how you come on in your sermon ; mine ("good easy man") is not *begun*, and I don't know when it will—but I have a long year before me, till it be required.

I have thus, my dear Bob, sent you a sheet filled with very close and small letters, as you desired, and whether there be anything in it or no, still it is full.   Pay me *directly*, I repeat it. Meantime I am, till I hear from you, my dear sir, yours truly,   THOMAS CARLYLE.

Have you read Shakespear ?   If you have not, then I desire you, read it directly, and tell me what you think of him—which is his master-piece.   He is always excellent.

The following passage from Carlyle's *Re-miniscences*, vol. i. p. 89, illustrates the pre-ceding letter and those which immediately follow :—

"It was now the winter of 1815.   I had myself been in Edinburgh College ; and above a year ago had duly quitted it ; had got (by competition at Dumfries, summer 1814) to

be 'Mathematical Master' in Annan Academy, with some
potential outlook on Divinity as ultimatum (a rural 'Divinity
Student' visiting Edinburgh for a few days each year, and
'delivering' certain 'discourses '). Six years of that would
bring you to the church-*gate*, as four years of continuous
'Divinity Hall' would ; unlucky only that, in my case, I
had never had the least enthusiasm for the business (and
there were even grave prohibitive doubts more and more
rising ahead) : both branches of my situation flatly contra-
dictory to all ideals or wishes of mine ; especially the Annan
one, as the closely actual and the daily and hourly pressing
on me, while the other lay theoretic, still well ahead, and
perhaps avoidable. One attraction, one only, there was in
my Annan business. I was supporting myself (even saving
some few pounds of my poor £60 or £70 annually, against a
rainy day), and not a burden to my ever-generous father any
more ; but in all other points of view I was abundantly
lonesome, uncomfortable, and out of place there ; . . . in
short, thoroughly detested my function and position, though
understood to be honestly doing the duties of it ; and held
for solacement and company to the few books I could
command, and an accidental friend or two I had in the
neighbourhood (Mr. Church and his wife, of Hitchill ; Rev.
Henry Duncan, of Ruthwell, and ditto ; these were the two
bright and brightest houses for me. My thanks to them,
now and always !) As to my schoolmaster function, it was
never said that I *misdid* it much ('a clear and correct'
expositor and enforcer) ; but from the first, especially with
such adjuncts, I disliked it, and by swift degrees grew to
hate it more and more. Some four years in all I had of it ;
two in Annan, two in Kirkcaldy (under much improved
social accompaniments) ; and at the end, my solitary
desperate conclusion was fixed, That I, for my own part,

would prefer to perish in the ditch, if necessary, rather than continue living by such a trade :—and peremptorily gave it up accordingly."

III.—To Mr. ROBERT MITCHELL, Linlithgow.

MOUNT ANNAN, 18*th October* 1814.

MY DEAR MITCHELL—When I look at the date of your last elegant and endearing letter, I feel a throb of something approaching to *remorse* for the suspicion of ingratitude and inconstancy which you (if you thought of me at all) must have entertained of me, for my apparently unaccountable neglect of a correspondence which I had been the first to solicit, and the most eager to cultivate. I hope, however, that when you shall have heard " the story of my woes "—that is, my history for the last four months, you will be ready to grant me your forgiveness, and to receive me once more into your good graces.

Some three or four days after I received your lucubrations, an advertisement appeared in the newspapers for a Mathematical Teacher in the Annan Academy ;—the place is worth about £70 a year—and is respectable enough ; my friends, therefore, were anxious for my becoming a candidate. Having been favoured with a letter of recommendation from Mr. Leslie,[1] I *did* apply, and was informed that the candidates must undergo a comparative trial at Dumfries in the course of a few days, and that, in course, I must repair thither. Not to detain you with all the tribulations and heart-burnings I went through, it will be sufficient to inform you that I and another man having been examined by Mr. White,[2] I was preferred, and told I must enter on my office *next day*. This, you see, was quick work—but you have not heard all. General Dirom came to reside at Mount Annan towards the end of June, and two of his boys, learning Greek, Latin, and Mathematics, were consigned to my care. You can conceive the hurry and trepidation attendant upon obtaining and entering upon a new situation. You can conceive me

[1] The eminent John Leslie, Professor of Mathematics in the University of Edinburgh.

[2] Thomas White, Rector of the Academy at Dumfries, an excellent mathematician.

just thinking of a subject for a *reverie* for *your* perusal, and a new engagement knocking all my *reveries* on the head, and telling me that for four months I must lead the life of a *Mill-horse*—you can conceive all this, and can you help pardoning me? The truth is, scarcely a day these three months has passed over my head, but I have reproached myself for ingratitude to my friend, to the companion of my studies, my speculations and *perpendings* (sweet *bygane times!*); and, strange as it may seem, every day I have again *put off*. "Pro-crastination is the thief of time," and I am persuaded that nothing but the fear of your quitting my correspondence in disgust could have *aroused me*. I have at length *determined*, "though it were when I should sleep," to write you—and here am I scribbling away at midnight your most humble servant.

My dear Mitchell, I entreat you to *sustain* this excuse, for indeed none of the circumstances are exaggerated,—and to rest assured that the friendship of a son of genius, of similar pursuits, of kindred sentiments, and congenial spirit with myself, is too highly prized to be even apparently neglected, except upon the most imperious necessity. Believe me I shall be most unhappy if this excuse don't satisfy you, and will come under any terms rather than forfeit my right to a letter *directly*. After this long preamble you are not to expect that I, all *jaded* as I am, can even attempt to *amuse* you this bout, but, my dear Boy, send me a letter informing me that you are reconciled, and I'll warrant you receive a letter full of— *quirk* and *oddity*, covered thick and threefold with mirth—*humour*—WIT, and the several other appendages requisite for forming an unexceptionable *morçeau d'eloquence et d'esprit:* but at present 'tis out of the question to expect anything more spirited than a *last will*, or more witty than a *Methodist tract*. But let me get forward as I may.

In seriousness your Mathematical investigations are excellent. Your demonstration of the property of the circle is really neat (I at least should think so, for on reading your enunciation I set to work and brought out a demon-

stration of the property, which I was both
disappointed and pleased to find the SAME AS
YOURS) : but it is the trisection of the arc that
I *admire ;* it is indeed *acutely* and *beautifully*
handled. " But thereby hangs a tale." I did
not tell you that when I left Edinburgh for
Dumfries I put your paper in my pocket—and
whilst my right worthy *compagnons de voyage*
(for I came in the Mail from Moffat) were
sunk in politics, post-horses, farming, etc., I
took out my friend's theorem, and leaving the
base clod-hoppers to welter on among drains
and dunghills and bullocks and balances of
power, 'I entered Dumfries *wholly disengaged
from sublunary things ;* and well-nigh persuaded
that an angle *might* be trisected. I went next
morning to breakfast with Mr. White, and in
the course of our conversation, happening to
mention the trisection of an angle, " I have in
my pocket," said I, " the result of an ingenious
young friend and fellow-student's attempts on
that subject. 'Tis here." Mr. W. had no
sooner cast his eye upon your diagram than,
starting up and uttering a wildly-accented

"aye!!" he left the room. He soon dissipated the mystery by returning with an armful of dun aged manuscripts; he desired me to look at one of them, and I *was* surprised to see *the same property*. He complained bitterly that *Mr. Leslie had showed it you* and never mentioned *his* name! I assured him that it was an original on your part; but in vain. "'Tis *impossible!*" was his reply: I could not but feel rather vain, that I had a friend who had found out properties of which a veteran like White was proud.

By the way, could not we, think you, contrive to continue this mode of interchanging our lucubrations? 'Tis a project I like vastly, and from which I had promised myself much instruction, as well as entertainment. I have on hand (I should rather say *in head*) an explanation of the *rainbow*, together with some other *bagatelles* which I could send you—if I could think of any mode of conveyance. Could you devise no plan of regular communication? In Winter, at least, they could be conveyed to and from Edinburgh, *free of expense*, in some honest

student's box. Let me have your ideas on the
subject. Our college comrades, honest *Davie*,
and the *son of cat-gut*—where are they? I had
a hint, and only a hint, that Davie had beaten
his *forceps* into *pitch-forks*,—and his *scalpels*
into *pruning-hooks*—that is to say—had commenced plough-man. Pray tell me is it true?
And has Andrew quitted Corstorphine?

.   .   .   .   .   .

What Books have you been perusing? and
how did you like Shakespeare? Since I saw
you I have toiled through many a thick octavo
—many of them to little purpose. Byron's—
and Scott's *Poems* [I have read] and must
admire,—though you recollect, *we* used to give
Campbell a decided preference, and I still
think, with justice. Have you ever seen
Hoole's *Tasso*? I have among many others—
read, *it*, *Leonidas*, the *Epigoniad*,[1] *Oberon*,[2]
Savage's *Poems*, etc. Miss Porter's *Scottish
Chiefs*, and *Waverley* have been the principal

[1] A happily forgotten Epic by a Scotchman, Dr. William
Wilkie. Hume professed great admiration for it, and Carlyle
may have read it as a patriotic duty.

[2] Doubtless Sotheby's version of Wieland's *Oberon*.

of my Novels. With regard to *Waverley*[1] I
cannot help remarking that in my opinion it is
the best novel that has been published these
thirty years. The characters of Ebenezer
Cruickshanks mine host of the Garter,[2] the
Reverend Mr. Goukthrapple and Squire Brad-
wardine display a Cervantic vein of humour
which has seldom been surpassed—whilst the
descriptions of the gloomy caverns of the
Highlands, and the delineations of the apathic
Callum Beg and enterprising Vich Ian Vohr,
show a richness of Scottean colouring which
few have equalled. Give me your opinion of
it if you have read it;—and if not—endeavour
by all means to procure it.

My sermon *is* pretty much in the same style
as yours *was* at the date of your last letter—
with this difference—I don't know quite so well
in what part of the Bible it is. My sentiments
on the Clerical profession are like yours, mostly
of the unfavourable kind. Where would be

---

[1] *Waverley* was published in 1814.
[2] Not of the " Garter," but of the " Seven-Branched Golden
Candlestick."

the harm, should we both stop? "The best-
concerted schemes o' mice an' men gang aft
aglee!" I intended to have said something of
the bigoted scepticism of Hume—but as I am
convinced you see through his specious sophisms
and detect his blind *prejudice* in *favour* of
infidelity, I shall defer it. At any rate I have
not room, and therefore *must* wait.

Now, my dear Bob, let me see you behave
as you ought, and send me a long letter, and I
promise it *shall* be answered punctually if I
keep my health. In sooth, I shall expect an
answer to this *Chaos* of a letter (which hurry,
etc., and your good-nature will excuse) within
fourteen days from the date hereof; so be
punctual.

Pray do write me directly an account of all
your transactions, adventures, misfortunes, loves,
and hates. I am close upon the bottom of my
sheet, otherwise I would say some *fine thing* on
the "Charms of Friendship;" but I trust, my
dear Mitchell, *we can both feel* the joys arising
from the commerce of kindred sentiments and
congenial minds.

Direct to me at Annan Academy—*quick.*

Need I add how sincerely I am, my dear Mit., yours,

THOMAS CARLYLE.

IV.—To Mr. ROBERT MITCHELL, Ruthwell Manse.

MOUNT ANNAN, 24*th October* 1814.

MY DEAR MITCHELL—Nothing could exceed my pleasure at receiving your obliging and entertaining, though laconic epistle. I hope, however, I need not tell you that the *foolishness* of your letter was not the cause of my long silence. You should know enough of me by this time, to be aware that your letter was altogether according to my heart and fancy,—and accordingly I had, the other day, written a right dolorous and woe-be-gone memorial, in which I humbly showed, that I had been over head and ears in business—that adventures and misventures and trials and tribulations had so crowded upon me that my sap and substance was evaporated ; I represented — but what matters what I represented—since with all its

stains and blotches on it you will assuredly see
it—after it shall have performed *the tour of
Scotland,* for (O luckless man!) it was sent off
to Linlithgow last Wednesday, exactly the day
before I heard from Little Johnson (Corrie)
that you had come to Ruthwell! "Say shall —
thine anger then abate, upon consideration of
egregious ink-shed?" . . .

So Andrew is still at Gogar. I join right
heartily in your short but fervent petition for
his consolation. Davie and I, after convoying
[you] that day on your way to Lithgow —
struck across the fields and paid him a visit,
and after considerable trouble were admitted
into his *grotto* or *cavern* or CRUI.[1] The most
considerable of his movables were a chair wanting a back, a joint-stool, eight potatoes, and
a pot of brimstone: but to give you any idea
of the situation and contours of this den,—to
represent to you the stern and doughty appearance of its innocent inhabitant,—much more to
make you *sensible* of the "*rancorous* com—
pound of villainous smells" that on all sides

[1] Sty, hog-pen.

"offended nostril," is impossible. The *tout-ensemble* was dank and dreary, and

Dark as was Chaos e're the infant Sun was roll'd together,
Or had tried his beams athwart the gloom profound.

And yet Andrew, good easy man! shrugging up his shoulders, told us "*he was living like the ancients.*" With all his oddity he is a good, honest lad. And Davie too! Well, peace be with ye, good kind-hearted souls!

Clint, poor man, hath taken unto himself a wife, and at this time sojourneth in the ancient burgh of Lochmaben. Hill is at Middlebie, *in statu quo;* and James Johnstone is lately returned from the Selkirk hall. Alas! poor creatures, we are all dispersing towards the four winds of heaven—and embarking on life's wide ocean—and how shall we each steer his little bark through all the shoals and hurricanes that lie before us, where so many stately Gallies have foundered on the passage! 'Tis a bleak look-out, my dear Mit.—but though the greasy *sons of pudding* may pass us by with all the *conscious dignity* of beings of a higher and a *fatter* order, yet however humble be our lot, 'tis comfortable to think that—

> Justum et tenacem propositi virum,
> Non civium ardor prava jubentium,
> Non vultus instantis tyranni
> Mente quatit solida . . .
> Si fractus illabatur orbis
> Impavidum ferient ruinæ.

But truce! whither am I running? let us quit moralising.

If ever you receive that 'foresaid stray-epistle you will see that even while I thought you at Linlithgow, I had not quitted the plan of interchanging the results of our speculations, —and ·you may easily imagine, I will not relinquish my expectations of your concurrence with my proposals now that you are within seven miles of me. In truth, I think it could not fail of being advantageous and entertaining to us both. What do *you* think of it? Have you any articles of the *spin-brain* manufacture by you at present? For *me*, poor soul, I have been kept like unto a cock-on-a-spit these four months, with hardly time to breathe, much less to *think*. Take an instance,—I am at this present—cold stormy midnight—*scratching* and writing what I at times think *you* will consider a letter—with a *nose*, saving the mark, I daresay as blue as indigo, and I *do* say as cold as an icicle,—with the consoling reflection, however, that when I *do* get to bed I shall not be disturbed till six in the morning. How can I *think?* But let not this interrupt *your* communications; General Dirom will be away in the course of four weeks or so, and then I shall have more time.

Mr. Duncan left Mount Annan this morning; and having invited me to Ruthwell Manse—you may expect to see me in the course of a week or two some Saturday afternoon, when, my dear Bob, we shall talk over our *bygane days o' auld lang syne*, and perhaps have another bout at PERPENDING. Tuesday must bring me a letter brimful of all things— or else—for now *you* are in *my* debt. Let me have all your theories and trials and temptations and hypotheses. Are you disengaged on Saturdays? for if I should come out and find you—But lo! I am at the bottom of my paper—

and right fortunate is it for both—for in sooth so cold and *kiestless*[1] am I,—in a short time I should have been absolutely preaching. I will not ask your pardon for this motley farrago,—rejoice it is not worse. Write me as punctually at the day appointed, as punctually as it is in human nature to write—pass not sentence of excommunication on me—and be assured, I remain, my dear old Mit., your sincere friend (and semi-frozen servant),

THOMAS CARLYLE.

.   .   .   .   .   .

V.—To Mr. R. MITCHELL, Ruthwell Manse.

ANNAN, 11*th January* 1815.

MY DEAR MITCHELL—I must send a cover to a long farrago of stuff, and in order to save appearances, and to avert the dire threats of bonds and imprisonment which you so liberally deal out in your last letter,—I have sat down to give you an account of my life and conversation since I saw you last. Nothing material

1 Spiritless, inert.

happened to me in town after your parting from
me,—and except purchasing Campbell's *Poems*,
and transacting *quelques petites affaires* which it
is needless to trouble you with, and getting my
lungs well-nigh suffocated with the *foul air*, and
the *tympanum* of my ears nearly torn to pieces
with the war-whoops of the Edinburgh *Hogma-
nay*[1]-night, I might have been said to be station-
ary.   On Sunday morning I left Edinburgh on
the outside of the coach, like you, in the gayest
humour in the world, but before riding half a
dozen miles the "biting breezes" of the East
began to disturb me, and notwithstanding the
consolation I derived from a shaggy greatcoat,
and from comparing the *dread-nought* appearance of our guard (who to a natural obesity of
body altogether hyperbolical, had added the
adventitious aids of 2738·5 cubic inches of solid
cloth and leather in the form of a tremendous
impenetrable roquelaure, and surmounted the
whole of this terror-striking apparatus with an
awful broad-brimmed hat :—displacing as he
stood not less than twelve solid feet of air) with

[1] The last day of the year.

the pitiful woe-worn visages of two fellow-
travellers, whose livid noses and rattling teeth
proclaimed (one would have thought) that the
hour of their dissolution was at hand,—notwithstanding all this, by the time we reached Hair-
stanes, I was right thankful to get inside of the
"leathern-conveniency,"—where I continued all
the way to Moffat. I made shift to fall into
a kind of *torpor* whilst travelling down the
Tweed—at least to shut my eyes upon the
bleak and barren uniformity of its ash-grey
hills, till on our vehicle's suddenly stopping, I
thrust out my head, and descried *Tweed Shaws.*
Recollecting your and my horrid circumstances
a few days before, I could not help silently
ejaculating a fervent prayer that I might *never*
again be under the necessity of passing a night
in the residence of the men of Tinwald, nor of
ever passing another instant of my existence
with the RED CUDDY[1] of Moffat. But my paper
is almost done, and only half my journey completed. "Brief therefore will I be." I left
Moffat at midnight in the Glasgow mail—and

[1] *Cuddy*, diminutive of Cuthbert = jackass.

having arrived at home at about four o'clock—
proceeded to Annan on Tuesday morning—safe
and sound after all my perils and tribulations.
If you can draw any "*soul-comforting reflections*" from this, much good may they do you—
and meantime I remain, your (servant to command),
                                    THOMAS CARLYLE.

2 o'clock Thursday morning.

VI.—To Mr. R. MITCHELL, Ruthwell Manse.

ANNAN, 25*th March* 1815.

MY DEAR BOB—At sundry times, and in
divers ways, I have pondered upon a project I
had formed of sending you a letter to arouse
you, if possible, from the state of torpor in
which, of late, to my unspeakable regret your
faculties were benumbed. You are obliged to
me for my intentions, and though tribulations of
various sorts have prevented me from putting
them in execution, you are not the less obliged
on that account. You are a happy fellow, Mit.,
to be allowed to sit under your vine and under

your fig-tree, quietly ruminating on your thirty-nine articles, with none to make you afraid. And how could you be so cruel as to mention those heart-breaking discourses ?   How, or when, or wherewithal are they to be made ! In sobriety, that *putting off*, and that *dissipation of studies* is a serious evil.   A thousand times have I lamented that hop-skip-and-jump disposition of mine which is perpetually prompting me to fly off at a tangent from whatever I am engaged in.   Your " auricular confession " owns the same propensity ; and I begin to think it is a fault of *every* mind—which effort alone can cure.   I could be *metaphysical* perhaps, but you will be better satisfied with an example : It was but yesternight that I, your most obedient servant, became all at once sensible of *the importance of present time*, and having brought out my *accoutrements*, set right doughtily to the composition of my *Exegesis*.   I began with alacrity of soul, and had finished the fourth line when I made a—dead halt !   One cannot long be idle—you will not wonder that I took up the first book that came in my way—

and though it was the dullest of all dull books, yet by a fatality attendant on those things, I could not give it up. It purported to be a "history of a lover," showing how Cecilia (somebody), being poor but honest, went to Paris with some Brandy Irish Dowager (of Tipperary), and was much astounded at their goings on, yet very much liked by the *beaux*. Showing how after divers trials and temptations she married with a lord (something) who had been a very great rascal in his early days, but was now become a most delectable personage; how they lived in great harmony of souls, till the honest man riding one day on some wold, and happening to fall from his beast in presence of this notable lady, she fell into hysterics or convulsions, and was taken home in a woeful plight, where she loitered on till she was "brought to bed," when she took her leave of the good-man and all the world. Would you believe me, I read and read this horrid story, and might have been reading yet had not a most dolorous ode to Matrimonial—no "Monody on the-death of a beloved, etc." compelled me to throw past the book, and set to writing you a letter. Tell *me* not again of "Jacks-of-all-trades," you are a King of a student compared with me.

You are charitable enough to suppose that my head is full of ideas; your good-nature misleads you. I have indeed had ideas, and strange ones too, since I wrote you; but like many other remarkable ideas, they have had the fortune to evaporate as soon as produced. Mathematics I have absolutely never thought on, excepting some trifles from the *Ladies' and Gentlemen's Diary*, which I shall have conscience enough not to trouble you with at present. Great and manifold are the books I have read since I saw you. You recommended *Thaddeus of Warsaw* long ago, you may remember,—and the work in my judgment fully deserves it. Miss Porter has no wit, she invariably bungles a picture of the conversation of ordinary persons whenever she attempts it. Why does she delight in unfolding the forward weaknesses of the *female* heart, and making even Mary Beaufort love first? Yet with all her deficiencies she is interesting: never failing to excite our sympathy, though she cannot rank with our Fieldings or Smolletts. She infinitely surpasses the insipid froth of

"The mob of Gentlemen, who write with ease."

As an extraordinary instance of perseverance, I must mention my having read *Cicero de Officiis.*[1] You must read it too, Bob; you will get through it in a week, and cannot think your time misspent. It consists of letters addressed to his son, and if we compare the steady, affectionate, unbending precepts of the venerable Roman with the only work of a similar kind in our own times, *Chesterfield's*

---

[1] Carlyle seems to have been reading a good deal in Cicero about this time. In a letter written in April of this year to his friend Thomas Murray, he says: "But the book I am most pleased with is Cicero, *de Finibus;* not that there is much new discussion in it, but his manner is so easy and elegant; and besides, there is such a charm connected with attending to the feelings and principles of a man over whom 'the tide of years has rolled.' We are entertained even with a common sentiment; and when we meet with a truth which we ourselves had previously discovered, we are delighted with the idea that *our* minds are similar to that of the venerable Roman."

Advice, we shall blush for the eighteenth century!

But the most extraordinary production of any I have seen these many days, is *La Pucelle d'Orléans*, an Epic by Voltaire. This' Mock-Heroic illustrates several things. First, that the French held Voltaire a sort of demigod; secondly (and consequently), that they were wrong in so doing; and thirdly, that the said Voltaire is the most impudent, blaspheming, libidinous blackguard that ever lived. As proof of the first take the following specimen of French ingenuousness, from the preface by the Editor. After affirming that the poem is Voltaire's, he observes that " Personne n'a été la dupe du desaveu qu'il a fait de ce poëme, dans une lettre à Messieurs de l'Académie Française. Sa véracité est connue depuis longtemps. Tout le monde sçait, qu'affirmer ou nier, selon les temps, les lieux, les convenances fut toujours une de ses maximes favorites ; et en vérité, un homme aussi extraordinaire, doit bien avoir des principes qui lui soient propres." Happy great man! Peace be to him and his "principes qui

lui soient propres!"   An epigrammatist sagely
remarks—

> " C'est du Voltaire—et tout est beau,
>   Tout plait chez lui, jusqu'au *blasphème.*"

To illustrate the third proposition—take any
part of the poem—it is infinitely inferior in
point of wit to *Hudibras*—yet were we not
continually shocked with some indecent, vicious,
or profane illusion, it would not be unentertain-
ing.   There is a description of the Temple of
Fame, something in the spirit of Swift, which
I would send had I room.   The following [is
a] new representation of the miseries of the
builders of Babel—

> " Sitôt qu'un d'eux à boire demandait,
>   *Plâtre* ou *mortier* d'abord on lui donnait."

Add that it is professedly intended "pour
les jeunes demoiselles."   I most heartily "wish
them luck o' the prize, man!"   I have also read
—but hold thy hand thou wayward mortal!
consign not to the flames this ill-fated scrawl!—
it is egotistical, it is nonsensical—and I speak
it with a sigh—it is dull!   Yet burn it not—if

a condition bordering on coma, if an endless
series of misfortunes and south-west winds
which have almost obliterated my spirit, cannot
excuse me, think for thine own sake—is there
not many a dulcet precept still slumbering at
the bottom of my inkhorn, which it will do thy
heart good to receive ?   Think and read !—
Which of ye, ye long-headed ones of the earth,
ever dreamt that little *Nap*, tired of fretting
out his heart in Elba, would rise Phœnix-like,
disdaining "the limits of his little reign," and
once more front the world—determined to die
"with harness on his back!"   Your calculations
are ruined, for *Nap* is on the field!   And now
poor d——l, when so many men that wield
sceptres and paving-shovels—when so many
people that have diadems and gridirons are
combined against thee—why should *I* be thine
enemy ?   No! fight thine own battle, and come
what speed thou mayest for me.   And yet I
fear, my little fellow, thou art upon slippery ice,
still thou hast many a trick, and with more
truth than it was ever said of another, may it
be said of thee,

" Ton âme impie, inflexible, implacable,
Dans les enfers vaudra braver le Diable ! "
                              VOLTAIRE.[1]

But I must finish this *badinage*—and assure you,
my dear Mit., that I never was more serious
than when I add that I am yours most sincerely,

THOMAS CARLYLE.

If you don't write, sir, instantaneously—it is
almost two o'clock, and I writing the most con-
founded nonsense merely to provoke an answer
—if you fail, I can't tell what to do with you.

Direct to me at James Gass', Cabinet maker,
Edmond St. For among my other adventures
it was destined that I should quarrel with a
Lancashire Jackall, which Mr. Kennedy keeps
by way of house-keeper, and consequently shift
my lodgings. Adieu, my dear Mit. Write immediately.

---

[1] " In the name of wonder," wrote Mitchell in his reply to
this letter, " why did you fill your letter with such blads
[*Anglice*, big pieces] of French ? Besides the enormous difficulty of translation, it keeps out some of your own *jeux-
d'esprit*, which are much more palatable to my taste than any
from the philosopher of Ferney."

VII.—To Mr. R. MITCHELL, Ruthwell Manse.

ANNAN, 24*th May* 1815.

MY DEAR MITCHELL—You ought to thank me for not writing you sooner. Buffeted as I have been, without ceasing, since I saw you, by innumerable squadrons of blue demons, my imaginations have been only the decoctions of ill-humour, and my letter must have been either a hyperbatavian tissue of dulness, or a string of complaints and imprecations unfit for the perusal of any person, more at ease in body than a gouty valetudinarian, or in mind than a *great man* on his way to Botany Bay. Not that the case is mended. Winds and rains, and crosses and losses have reduced a temper, naturally warm, to a state of caustic irritability, that renders me unfit for anything. " How weary, flat, stale, and unprofitable, seem to me all the uses of this world!" For, what are its inhabitants? Its great men and its little—its fat ones and its lean? From the courtier to the clodhopper—from the emperor to the dust-man—what are they all? Pitiful automatons—

despicable Yahoos—yea, they are altogether an unsufferable thing. " O ! for a lodge in some vast wilderness, some boundless contiguity of shade, where" the scowl of the purse-proud Nabob, the sneer and strut of the coxcomb, the bray of the ninny and the clodpole, "might never reach me more !" But truce to this philippic,—vexations like these affect only the poor, misguided, wandering misanthrope ; and (bless thy stars, my good Mitchell) thou art not of them.

The first article in the last *Quarterly Review* is on Stewart's second volume.[1] The wise men of London are earnest in their censures of "the metaphysical heresies" of their northern neigh-bours ; and notwithstanding the high admira-tion they pay to Stewart's talents, they differ from him in almost all his results, because they disbelieve his principles—the "first principles" of Dr. Reid. Their opinion (and they give no reasons), on a point of this nature, is of little consequence. All the prejudices natural to

[1] Dugald Stewart's *Elements of the Philosophy of the Human Mind.*

Englishmen they entertain in their full extent, and always modify their decisions accordingly. For my part, though far be it from me to attempt to disparage or vilipend this great man, I cannot help thinking that the perusal of his book has done me hurt. Perpetually talking about analysing perceptions, and retiring within one's self, and mighty improvements that we are to make—no one knows how,—I believe he will generally leave the mind of his reader crowded with disjointed notions and nondescript ideas—which the sooner he gets rid of, the better! I know you think differently; but *de gustibus non est disputandum;* and very probably, the fault is not with our Author, but his subject. . . . *Guy Mannering* is reviewed in the same number. Though we have still more reason to question their competency here, you will probably admit that "the Dutch boors of Mannering though never so well painted, must cause a class of sensations different from those excited by the Salvator banditti of *Waverley.*" Yet the only extract they give (the departure of the gypsies and Meg Merrilies' address to Ellangowan) is very much in the Salvator style.

I am glad you saw Lara, and am indebted⁻ for your account of it. I read the review of it in the *Quarterly Review* some time ago. Lara, it seems, is the identical Conrad, and Kaled no other than that same "dark-eyed slave," Gulnare, of whom such frequent mention is made in "The Corsair." The story appears to want *éclairissement.* What could become of the madcap Knight? And what was the meaning of that carcase in the river? Why did he raise the war-whoop in the lobby? Your solution of the last difficulty is too general; besides, had he really been *an-hungered*, the natural remedy was to visit the pantry.

I am highly indebted to you for Hume. I⁻ like his *Essays* better than anything I have read these many days. He has prejudices, he does maintain errors,—but he defends his posi- tions with so much ingenuity, that one would be almost sorry to see him dislodged. His essays. on "Superstition and Enthusiasm," on "The Dignity and Meanness of Human Nature," and

several others, are in my opinion admirable
both in matter and manner, particularly the
first, where his conclusions might be verified by
instances with which we are all acquainted.
The manner, indeed, of all is excellent; the
highest and most difficult effect of art—the
appearance of its absence—appears throughout.
But many of his opinions are not to be adopted.
How odd does it look, for instance, to refer *all*
the modifications of "national character" to the
influence of moral causes. Might it not be
asserted with some plausibility, that, even those
which he denominates moral causes, originate
from physical circumstances? Whence but
from the perpetual contemplation of his dreary
glaciers and rugged glens, from his dismal
broodings in his long and almost solitary
nights, has the Scandinavian conceived his
ferocious Odin, and his horrid "spectres of the
deep"? Compare this with the copper-castle
and celestial gardens of the Arabians—and we
must admit that physical causes *have* an influence on man. I read *The Epicurean, The
Stoic, The Platonist*, and *The Sceptic* under

some disadvantage. They are perhaps rather clumsily executed—and the idea of David Hume declaiming, nay of David Hume *making love*, appears not less grotesque than would that of [*seal covers*] or [*seal covers*] dancing a French cotillon. As a whole, however, I am delighted with the book, and if you can want it, I shall moreover give it a second perusal. I have got to the end of this rambling letter, and I think in rather better spirits than I commenced. Why did you not write me again ere this ? You knew my woful plight, and ought to have had compassion on my infirmities. To make amends, I allow you a week, and within that time you are to send me a most spirit-stirring epistle. Abuse me, if you will, for my vagaries, only be pithy, and be speedy too.

I am confidently informed that the man of music, Andrew, is still bent upon exploring the new world. Nay, it is stated by his intended comrade (who has now wisely preferred making wheel-barrows at Castle-Milk, and living as his fathers did, to going to labour he knows not where, and feed upon he knows not what) that

Andrew's accoutrements—his box—was on its way to Greenock a fortnight ago! The Yankees are long-headed personages, and Andrew is a simple man. But he can fiddle, he can dig, and to beg he is not ashamed. You know what *you must do*, Bob, before Thursday first— *be pithy*—nothing but pepper and salt will suit me in my present humour.—My dear Mit., ever yours,

THOMAS CARLYLE.

VIII.—To Mr. ROBERT MITCHELL, Ruthwell Manse.

ANNAN, 14*th June* 1815.

MY DEAR BOB—Your letter of the 31st May gave me a great deal of pleasure. I had heard a sort of vague account that you were sick; and I had formed the project of coming up to con- dole with you, when (it seems) you had so much need of condolence, buffeted as you have been by "ennui, torpor and hepatitis." It made me happy to learn that you had come to a "quietus"—and the only remark I shall make on the subject is—*be thankful* that such

moderate allowances of " Leech's bolus " were
able to produce the effect—for there are froward
creatures in the world, to make whose "quietus"
defies the power of anything less efficacious than
"a bare bodkin."

You take it upon you to scold me for not
calling as I went to Dumfries. But hear my
story, Mit. I was proceeding quietly from
Ecclefechan to Annan, without the smallest
intention of going on any such expedition, when
I met with Johnstone, and he advised me to
accompany him. We were obliged to use all
possible despatch for fear of being too late ; and
(before we got Jeffrey accoutred at Flosh, etc.
etc.) it being about eleven o'clock, I had
absolutely no time to see you, though I certainly intended it when I left Annan. Indeed,
I did see from the road, a tall lank figure per-
forming its gyrations round Ruthwell Church
with much solemnity : but whether it was
Mitchell, I know not. It was near two when
we got to Dumfries—and being consequently
prevented from getting within half a league of
St. Michael's—we saw the ceremony of laying

the stone,[1] exactly as well as if we had been in the grand square of Timbuctoo. Yet notwithstanding this—notwithstanding that all the scullions in Dumfriesshire were "let slip," notwithstanding the cantering and parading of the Ettrick Yeomen, notwithstanding the paper caps, the figured roquelaures, the magic-lanterns of free masonry, it was a striking scene. Scotland paying the tribute of well-earned honour to one of the noblest of her sons. It is a great pity that the monument will not be over his grave; many inconveniences ought to have been submitted to in order to gain this point. When I passed Ruthwell again, it was after midnight, so that you have nothing to blame me for on that score.

I could not send you the *Review*, for the man of whom I had borrowed it had got it again, and lent it to another. If I can get it again at any time, I will send it you. Have you seen the last *Edinburgh Review?* There are several promising articles in it—Scott's

---

[1] The foundation stone of the monument to Burns.

"Lord of the Isles," "Standard Novels," "Lewis' and Clarke's Travels up the Missouri " (of which a most delectable account is given in the *Quarterly*), " Joanna Southcott," etc. etc. I have been revising Akenside since I saw you. He possesses a warm imagination and great strength and beauty of diction. His poem, you know, does not, like Campbell's " Hope," consist of a number of little incidents told in an interesting manner, and selected to illustrate his positions,—it is little else than a moral declamation. Nevertheless I like it. Akenside was an enthusiastic admirer of the ancient republics and of the ancient philosophers. He thought highly of Lord Shaftesbury's principles, and had a bad opinion of Scotsmen. For this last peculiarity he has been severely caricatured by Smollett in his *Peregrine Pickle*, under the character of the fantastic English doctor in France. When we mention Shaftesbury, is his book in your possession, and can you let me have a reading of it ? I am inclined to suppose that the prevalence of infidelity is on the decline. Pride will often overturn what reason

had attempted in vain, and when the carrion
and offal of human nature begin to adopt the
tenets of our sages, we look for something new.
What leads me to say this is that I have heard
lately that there are in Middlebie sundry
cunning workmen, some skilled in the intri-
cacies of the loom, some acquainted with the
operations of the lapstone, who are *notable
deists*—nay, several aspire to taste the sublime
delights of *Atheism!* Now, when creatures
superior in so few respects (inferior in so many)
to the cow that browses on their hills, begin to
tread upon the heels of the wise ones of the
earth, the hue and cry about freedom from
popular errors, defiance of vulgar prejudices,
glory of daring to follow truth, though alone,
etc. etc. etc., is annihilated, and "all the rest
is leather and prunella." But we will talk on
those subjects afterwards.

Give my best respects to Mr. and Mrs.
Duncan, and mention that I intend to have the
pleasure of seeing them in a short time. I
cannot come first Saturday for many reasons.
I cannot come the next Saturday, for then is

Mr. Glen's[1] sacrament, and I believe I shall be constrained to go to sermon. There is nothing that I know of to hinder me the week after that, and if all things answer I shall likely see you then. Though I began this letter last night, I have been obliged to write the greatest part of it since twelve o'clock to-day. It is within three minutes of one—and I have no more time. Write me immediately and I will be punctual in answering. Your Irish play is an *unique* in its kind. I shall be. obliged to you for your *pun*. I have never heard it. Keep Blair till I come and seek him—and believe me to be—my dear Mitchell, yours sincerely,

THOMAS CARLYLE.

IX.—To Mr. MITCHELL, Ruthwell Manse.

ANNAN, 11*th December* 1815.

MY DEAR MITCHELL—I opened your last letter with fear and trembling. I expected

---

[1] In the *Reminiscences*, i. 107, is an account of Mr. Glen, " Burgher minister at Annan, with whom I had latterly boarded there, and been domestically very happy in comparison."

nothing but reproaches—when lo! my sins are
laid upon the back of the unoffending Post-
John, and I am never blamed.   Indeed,
Mitchell, you have been too good : and I look
for nothing but that you will be ready to slay
me when you come to know that I have never
written you at all.   I beseech you let not your
wrath be kindled.   Stay till you have heard
my piteous circumstances—and I am persuaded
you will pardon me.   I might justly preface
my account with an *infandum regina*, but to-
proceed without ornament.   " Ye probably may
not know those lines of *Scaliger* (applied to-
dictionary-makers, and *mutatis mutandis* to
dictionary-users)—

> Si quem dura manet sententia judicis olim
>
> .   .   .   .   .   .
>
> Lexica contexat, nam cætera, quid moror? omnes
> Pœnarum facies hic labor unus habet."

You certainly imagine I am got terribly learned
since I saw you.   But fair and softly—I know
nothing at all about honest Scaliger ; and
" those lines" of his are, I believe, none of
the most honestly come by.   I conveyed them

(*convey* the wise it call) from Morell's preface
to Ainsworth's Dictionary,—a preface, I may
observe, the most strongly impregnated with
pedantry of any I ever read. But once more
let me proceed—"those lines of Scaliger" and
many other "lines," are applicable to me—as
you shall presently hear. After parting from
you at Ruthwell I consumed the remainder of
our vacation in sundry idle projects : one of
which was—going to Dumfries, and suffering
"the pain of three intolerable deaths" for the
purpose of hearing certain wise and faithful
counsellors display their eloquence at the
circuit trials. When I returned to Annan, it
occurred to me that it would be proper to see
what had become of my Hall discourses. It
occurred to me, much about the same time,
that it would be proper to study Rumford's
Essays, Mackenzie's *Travels*, Humboldt's *New
Spain*, Berkeley's *Principles of Knowledge*,
Stewart's *Essays*, Simson's *Fluxions*, etc. etc.
etc. It was some great man's advice to every
person in a hurry—never to do more than one
thing at a time. Judge what progress I must

have made when I engaged in half-a-dozen.
Manufacturing *theses*—wrestling with lexicons,
chemical experiments, Scotch philosophy and
Berkeleian Metaphysics—I have scarcely sufficient strength left to write you even now.
Upon consideration, therefore, of these egregious labours—I hope, you cannot refuse to
forgive me.

I am anxious to consult you about going to
Edinburgh this winter. I have already partly
told you that I have been making my *Exegesis.*—
It is now nearly finished ;—and truly a most
delectable production it is—but of this some
other time. I wrote to Murray in great haste,
to commission me a day, and it seems, I am
engaged to read on Friday the 22d current.
So that you see my time of setting out is
decided upon. You will ask me, why, since I
have almost come to a determination about my
fitness for the study of Divinity, why all this
mighty stir—why this ado—about " delivering "
a thesis—that in the mind's eye seems vile, and
in the nostril smells horrible? It is not because I have altered my sentiments about the

study of Theology : but principally because it came into my head to try what sort of an essay upon natural religion I could make. I have tried, and find accordingly that I can make one perfectly—" weary, flat, stale, and unprofitable," —but I am engaged, and must read it now. I do not expect yet that you will be able to tell me " whether the Sabbath is of divine institution "—but I do hope you have determined to go to Edinburgh this Winter along with me. If you have not I must not try to persuade you. You would suspect that my arguments arose from selfish motives,—and you would not be far from right ; for if you do not go, I shall be the most melancholy person imaginable. But I cannot help bringing to your recollection the possibility that you may change your opinion about becoming a clergyman, in which case your annual visit to Edinburgh will be of essential service. It does good, at any rate, by preventing that pity which certain people of grave minds are so disposed to bestow on every one that has not a fixed prospect in life ; and, over and above, it is pleasant to revisit one's *alma mater*. For these reasons, and for one (I confess it) as strong as any—that I shall be uncomfortable if you refuse—I earnestly wish you to determine upon this journey.

. . . . . .

You would have Landalls preaching last Saturday. How *does* he seem to do? "Doctrinal discourses"—true blue—I suppose. I have heard of a criticism passed by the late Dr. Finlay of Glasgow upon some eminent probationer; I know not whether it will apply. Upon being asked his opinion concerning the gentleman's oratorical powers, he made answer —"He hath a comely appearance, and hath attracted the notice of divers young men—and also of some young women." Have you heard that the very learned and very orthodox divine of Ochiltree is preparing to apply his polyglot stores to translating the New Testament— *Bonum, faustum, felix et fortunatum sit;* I am only sorry that I was obliged to become a subscriber—it is one pound four—if you take a thought of buying it, apply to me, and you shall have it for the odd silver.

I am obliged to you for your account of your Swiss visitants. With all imaginable deference to those who practise the sublime virtue of charity—I cannot altogether see what concern the peaceable inhabitants of Dumfriesshire have with the management of the convents situated among the glaciers of the Alps. Had the task of repairing their breaches been consigned to the *virtuosi* and the *cognoscenti* that frequent those regions, it might have been more befitting. But "all for the honour of England!"

Can you tell me whether Davie Graham is continuing to practise physic? He is a good honest lad ;—I am only afraid that the aphorisms of Celsus will not answer [for] the men of Tundergarth.[1] And Andrew!—alas! the green ocean is betwixt us! *Illi robur et aes triplex circa pectus erat.*

The fate of poor Andrew disposes one to be melancholy. What is to become of us, Mitchell? The period of our boyhood is past: and in a little while, if we live, behold we shall be bearded men! from whom wisdom

[1] A parish in Dumfriesshire.

and gravity will be required. It is now a year since we last visited Edinburgh. For my part, though I have laboured as I could in my vacation, can I say that I am either wiser or better in any perceptible degree? Out upon it! This—is a miserable world.

But let us quit moralising, and bethink us of our journey. You must write me on Thursday, that you will be ready at the time. I cannot think of any excuse you can plead with any chance of success. Are you afraid lest it hurt your health? Wrap yourself up in your roquelaure, and you can take no harm. You have been curling; and I am happy to believe, you have got round again. You certainly will come. I know not whether you will have heard that I am living with Mr. Glen since I came to Annan last. He is a real good man, as far as I can see; and Mrs. Glen is a fine cheerful woman,— so that upon the whole, I am not uncomfortable in my present circumstances. Most of the ministers that come here (no great number, let me be thankful) are curious bodies;—but I will speak of this elsewhere. In the meantime I must again repeat my petition—and hope that in a short time we shall be in Edinburgh together. —I am ever yours, my good Robin,

THOMAS CARLYLE.

"About Christmas time (1815)," writes Carlyle in his *Reminiscences* (i. 92), "I had gone with great pleasure to see Edinburgh again, and read in Divinity Hall a Latin discourse—'*Exegesis*' they call it there—on the question, '*Num detur religio naturalis?*' It was the second, and proved to be the last of my performances on that theatre. My first, an English sermon on the words, 'Before I was afflicted I went astray, but now,' etc. etc., a very weak and flowery sentimental piece, had been achieved in 1814, prior to or few months after my leaving for Annan. Piece second, too, I suppose, was weak enough, but I still remember the kind of innocent satisfaction I had in turning it into Latin in my solitude, and my slight and momentary (by no means deep or sincere) sense of pleasure in the bits of 'compliments' and flimsy 'approbations' from comrades and Professors on both these occasions. Before Christmas Day I had got rid of my Exegesis, and had still a week of holiday ahead, for old acquaintances and Edinburgh things, which was the real charm of my official errand thither."

X.—To Mr. ROBERT MITCHELL, Ruthwell Manse.

ANNAN, 15th February 1816.

MY DEAR MITCHELL—I know I should have written you a month ago, and I am not going

to take up your time with excuses. I have
indeed no excuse, except the perpetually forthcoming one—no time and no subject; and it
would be but aggravating my misconduct to
harangue you upon a topic that has been so
fully discussed by every writer of letters in
every age of the world. The truth is—I have
been a very torpid person of late. After undergoing the fatigues of a most uncomfortable
journey to Edinburgh, I returned with renewed
keenness to my old habits of seclusion and
repose; to reading when I was able, and when
I was not, to the forming of vain hopes and
silly projects, at which I have a peculiar knack.
But though I have not written to you, I have
had you often in my mind. Many a time
during my dreary pilgrimage to Edinburgh did
I solace myself with the hope of making you
merry with the recital of my adventures: a
hope which (as you are just going to see)
has, like many other hopes, proved utterly falla-
cious.

I left Ecclefechan on the evening of Tuesday the 19th December on the top of the

Glasgow mail. Little occurred worthy of
notice, till on my arrival at Moffat I discovered
among my fellow travellers, along with three
Lancashire cotton men, a fine species of the
popinjay—of whom, all that I can now say is,
that he was much shocked at seeing '*roos-beef
fo suppa*,' and expressed his grief and surprise
by several nondescript interjections ; that he was
unable to determine whether the fowl on the
table was a tame duck or wild, and thereupon
" did patiently incline " to the reasonings of an
ancient Scottish *gourmand* who at length succeeded in settling his mind upon this important
subject; and that upon my inquiring after the
news of the paper which he was reading, he
informed me that the *Aachdoocs* had returned
to England, and that (this he preluded by three
nods of satisfaction) the Prince Regent was
gone to Brighton.

The next day I had different objects to
speculate upon. I was mounted on the roof of
the coach in one of the most dismal days I ever
saw. It snowed heavily ; on our arrival at
Erickstane particularly, the roaring of the wind

and the ocean of drift carried with it, together with the bellowings of the distracted coachmen, and the outlandish warwhoops of two Irish doctors, who, along with myself, had dismounted till we should ascend the hill, formed a scene sufficiently wild. Of this I intended for your benefit, a very pathetic description,—as well as of the desolation of the Broughton Inn, where after a day of violent struggling we finally stopped. The kitchen, I remember, when I entered it, was filled with shepherds and carriers, and in the midst, like a breathing iceberg, stood our guard, describing with much emphasis the hardships of the day. Two female passengers had taken possession of another quarter of the house, and left the two Hibernians and me to pass the evening as we best were able. I did not by any means like my comrades. One of them (according to my conceptions)—but that he from time to time uttered certain acute sounds, and had a pair of little fiery eyes,—pretty much resembled an Egyptian mummy—a little meagre thing—skin apparently of the nature of parchment, and a complexion that seemed to have been produced by repeated immersion in strong decoctions of logwood. The other had a Kilmarnock bonnet. Both seemingly exceeding vain as well as stupid. I spent an unhappy evening. The mummy blew upon a German flute, and both talked of Antrim · and Drogheda, till I had come to a resolution of leaving them next morning at all hazards. I must not neglect to tell you of our dormitory;—finding there was only one bed allotted to us all, and wisely judging it prudent to make the best of a bad bargain, the mummy took possession of the middle. There is no· happiness, it is said, without alloy,—at least it proved so in this case; for although by this manœuvre the mummy received a comfortable proportion of warmth, yet the pressure of the Kilmarnock-bonnet-man upon his fragile sides seemed considerably to damp his enjoyment. It became at length so intolerable, indeed, as to compel him (after a desperate and ineffectual effort at release) to exclaim "*Marciful* Heaven preserve my *sowl*—what will become of me now?" The bitter whine in which this sentiment was uttered, and the sudden nature of such a preparation for dissolution (which, I might have inferred from the words, he expected forthwith) would in any other circumstances have overcome my gravity.

I left them next morning and set out on my forlorn expedition at four o'clock. It was truly an Icelandic scene. The wind had subsided during the night—all was silent—and the moon disclosed the dreary expanse of snow, which in many places was drifted into heaps of several feet in depth. I made but indifferent progress, —for after infinite flounderings (at one time literally up to the chin in snow) the sun rose upon me in the wolds of Linton. The track was entirely obliterated—and I suppose I was beginning to look silly enough, when I luckily descried a benevolent herdsman, who pointed out to me the road for Noblehouse,—from which I had deviated at the suggestion of a roadman, at whose cottage I had called, and who thought the higher road would be the clearer. I was glad to meet, at Noblehouse, with a Thomas Clark, Divinity student, whom I had known

in Edinburgh. He was preparing to mount
on horseback, and in the meantime introduced
me to a tall thin man, who, he said, intended to
walk to Edinburgh, having been long disappointed of a passage in the coach. There
was a stagnant placidity in this person's countenance, which inclined me to believe that he would
prove a sufficiently inoffensive companion. He
did turn out a very shallow man. He quest-
ioned the workmen whom we passed, with
much minuteness, concerning the state of the
rods that were before us; and conversed with
me upon no subject but that of the effects of
snow upon human bodies,—seeming particularly
anxious about the fate of his own *vile carrion.*—
He.tired; and I left him at Pennycuick sitting
with a kindred spirit, to all appearance a Peebles
weaver. I pursued my journey with unabating
velocity, and arrived at John Forrest's at last
about nine o'clock. I never was more happy
at seeing Edinburgh.

    I gave in my Discourse next day along with
Samuel Caven and another whom I did not
know. It was sustained without difficulty.

Caven's was a precious morsel. Its author, it
seems, is in some family in the East Country.
He is a jumbling person to speak with ; he
says "an infinite deal of nothing ; his reasons—
are as two grains of wheat hidden in two
bushels of chaff ; you shall seek all day ere you
find them, and when you have them, they are
not worth the search." But enough of him.
Our old college cronies have left Edinburgh
nearly to a man. Waugh still continues there
teaching and learning with all his might. I think
he was not quite so full of *calculi* as usual.
When we speak of *calculi*, I brought home
[some] mathematical books, which I must tell
you of. Bossut's *History of Mathematics*,
Wood's *Optics*, and Cunn's *Euclid* and Newton's *Principia* constitute my stock of this sort.
I got Lucan's *Pharsalia* also, and some little
extracts of Fenelon's *Dialogues des Morts*. If
there are any of these (except Newton, for
which you would be obliged to wait awhile)
that you wish to see—they are ready for you.
I had read Bossut before—and have not done—
much at him of late. Neither have I read any

quantity of Wood yet, having been nibbling at
the *Principia* (which with all my struggling, I
come but ill at understanding—indeed in some
places I don't understand it at all) ever since I
came home. Of Lucan I have not read above
seven lines. I saw Scott's *Waterloo* and *Guy
Mannering* when I was in Edinburgh. The
former has been so dreadfully abused already,
that I have nothing to add to the newspaper
puns, etc., with which it has been assailed.
There are (as Gray said of *The Castle of Indolence*) some good lines in it. I have far too
little room for speaking of Mannering's beauties
and defects at present. I will discuss it next
time I write, if I can find nothing better.

But I must close this long letter. I have,
as you see, devoted the night to writing my
adventures. You asked for *Cuddies* [1] and truly
I think I have driven you in an abundant
herd. There is still another person whom (if
he continues thus) you may think it reasonable

[1] "You must write me on your return from Edinburgh,
conveying the Doctor's criticism, and your adventures with all
the red *Cuddies* you may meet with."—Mitchell to Carlyle,
15th December 1815.

to add to the list. I beseech you give him quarter.

Notwithstanding my misdeeds, I will ask you for a letter—and a pretty early one too. You used yourself to be a sad correspondent you know, and ought therefore to have some conscience. I saw Landalls to-night—he says you have been unwell. I do hope, my good Mit., you are recovered. Tell me soon—and believe me ever, my dear Robin, yours sincerely,

THOS. CARLYLE.

XI.—To Mr. R. MITCHELL, Ruthwell Manse.

19th April 1816.

MY GOOD LAD—You must be aware that I have a right to rate you with considerable acrimony. Last time I saw you, you promised to send me a letter in a few days, yet several weeks have elapsed, and no letter has appeared. This is very blameworthy, but I need not scold you, for, in all probability, by the time you have studied the following disquisition—you will think yourself punished to the full. It is one of the theorems we were speaking of. I found it out some months ago; and an odd fancy struck me of turning the demonstration into the Latin tongue. My dialect of that language is, I doubt not, somewhat peculiar—and you may chance to find some difficulty in interpreting it. [Here followed the theorem in Latin.]

Such is the result of this investigation. Your theorem about the heptagon does not answer exactly: it is only a good approximation, as I perceive, and as you may perceive also, by consulting a table of sines and tangents, —I have forgot West's theorem about the circle and curves of the second order. It is no great matter surely, since I should not be able to demonstrate it, though I had it. I wish you would send it me notwithstanding.

I hope you have sustained no injury from your excursion to Edinburgh. I hope, too, that you spoke to Mr. Leslie concerning the books. If you have not procured [me] one, I must request you to lend me yours immediately for a short time, if you can do without it: for one of the boys has begun conics and I have lent him my book—and should like to have another copy of it by me, to consult at home. You must send me the theorem and book by Mr. Johnstone of Hitchill—who I understand is to be at Ruthwell to-day and who can easily bring them to Annan. A letter I am expecting with impatience. Yours ever,

THOMAS CARLYLE.

.   .   .   .   .   .

XII.—To Mr. R. MITCHELL, Ruthwell Manse.

ANNAN, *15th July* 1816.

MY DEAR FRIEND—I am greatly obliged to you for your letter. At present I had no great reason to expect it. Yet you must not suppose that I have wilfully neglected to write. It is two months since I set resolutely to work, determined to send you a very handsome letter without loss of time. And I had assuredly done so, had I not clearly perceived that it was not in my power to send you anything that could at all have interested you. Since that time I have been continually loading myself with unavailing reproaches; and I have begun to write at last, solely, lest by my silence I should offend you without remedy. You are therefore to expect nothing but a very useless letter from me; and dull as may be.

I am very sorry that you are so unhappy— it is my own case also, for I have been extremely melancholy during the last six weeks, upon many accounts. It is about ten days since I got rid of a severe inflammation of the throat, which confined me to the house for two weeks. During two or three days I was not able to speak plainly, and you will easily conceive that I passed my time very heavily. I endeavoured to read several things: I tried a book of modern Biography, *The British Plutarch;* but soon finding it to be a very miserable book, I shut it for good and all. I next opened the *Spectator*—and though his jaunty manner but ill accorded with my sulky humours, I toiled through a volume and a half with exemplary patience. Lastly, I had recourse to Lord Chesterfield's advice to his son; and I think I never before so distinctly saw the

pitiful disposition of this Lord. His directions
concerning washing the face and paring the
nails are indeed very praiseworthy: and I
should be content to see them printed in a
large type, and placed in frames above the
chimney-pieces of boarding schools, for the
purpose of enforcing the duties of cleanliness
upon the rising generation. But the flattery,
the dissimulation and paltry cunning that he is
perpetually recommending, leave one little
room to regret that Chesterfield was not his
father. Such was the result of my studies, in
my sickness ;—a result highly unfavourable to
those feelings of prostration before high birth
and weight of purse, which (many tell us) it is
so eminently the duty of all men to cultivate.
Indeed this is not the first time that I have
noticed in my mind a considerable tendency to—
undervalue the great ones of this world. Conscious that this sentiment proceeds in a considerable degree from my situation in life, I
sometimes endeavour to check it : but after all,
it requires little observation to teach us that
the Noble of Political society and the Noble of

Nature are different persons, in nine cases out of ten. I am also aware that Flaccus has said—that "*Principibus placuisse viris, non ultima laus est;*" but with great deference, I would submit to Flaccus, that the justness of his aphorism must depend upon the character of these same "Principes viri;" otherwise—it is easy to conceive a state of society, in which this *non ultima laus* of his must be very liberally shared with sycophants and pandars. But, I daresay, you have enough of these reflections. Turn we to something else:—I daresay I know as little of Navigation as you; and yet I do not feel great difficulty in explaining how Hamilton Moore[1] "resolves triangles on the surface of a Sphere into plane triangles." Hamilton Moore, honest man, gives himself no uneasiness about resolving his triangles—he takes them as he finds them —and considering them as plane triangles— solves his problems very comfortably. (I believe Leslie has a note in his *Trigonometry;*—

---

[1] The nineteenth edition of John Hamilton Moore's *Practi-cal Navigator* was published in London in 1814.

explaining the method of reducing the angles
of a spherical triangle to the plane triangle
formed by its chords). I readily agree with
you that Moore's rules are very defective :—his
remarks are often quite stupid—for instance,
his statement (noticed by Humboldt) that the—
attraction of a boat to a ship, or a ship to
a rock, is caused by *gravitation.* A similar
phenomenon may be witnessed by causing two
pieces of wood to float on a bowl of water—
and all men know that it is caused by capillary
attraction. I have never seen Keith's *Trigonometry,* and therefore cannot tell you anything
about it. I am glad to hear that you are getting forward so well with Homer—I know
almost nothing about him—having never read
anything but Pope's translation, and not above
a single book of the original, and that several
years ago. Indeed, I know very little of the
Greek at any rate. I have several times begun
to read Xenophon's *Anabasis* completely ; but
always gave it up in favour of something else.
You complain that nothing that you do leaves
a vestige behind it ;—what do you make of

Homer? For my part—I cannot well say
what I have been about since I wrote to you
last. Out of a considerable quantity of garbage
which I have allowed myself, at different inter-
tervals, to devour, I have only to mention
Crabbe's Poems as worthy of being read. In
addition to great powers of correct description,
he possesses all the sagacity of an anatomist
in searching into the stormy passions of the
human heart—and all the apathy of an anatomist in describing them. For the rest—I
continued reading Newton's *Principia* with
considerable perseverance and little success,—
till on arriving a short way into the third book
—I discovered that I had too little knowledge
of astronomy to understand his reasoning
rightly. And I forthwith sent to Edinburgh
for Delambre's *Abrégé d'Astronomie*, and in
the meantime betook myself to reading Wood's
Optics. I cannot say much about this book.
Its author intermeddles not with the abstruse
parts of the science,—such as the causes
of reflection and refraction,—the reason why
transparent bodies at given angles of incidence

reflect their light almost entirely (concerning which I meet with many learned details in the *Encyclopædia Britannica*), but contents himself with demonstrating, in a plain enough manner, the ordinary effects of plane and spherical mirrors,—and of lenses of various kinds,—applying his doctrines to the explanation of various optical instruments and remarkable phenomena.   But in truth, I know little about it; I read it with too great velocity.   I also read Keill's[1] *Introductio ad veram Physicam;* but I shall let it pass till next time I write. In fine, Delambre arrived; and I have read into his fourth *Leçon*—and like it greatly.   I intended to have told you some of his observations—but I would not overwhelm you with ennui all at once—and therefore I shall be silent at present.   *Ne quid nimis*, as the proverb saith.

On Friday we enjoyed the society of Brother Saffery of Salisbury—a solicitor (of

---

[1] John Keill was Savilian Professor at Oxford from 1709 to 1721.   He was a voluminous writer, and his works had value.

money) for the benefit of the Baptist Mission. I was rather disappointed in the appearance of this person. The name of a missionary suggests the idea of a lean and mortified ascetic—travelling with his staff and scrip—and with pious avarice, hoarding, for the behoof of his brethren, the scanty donations of a precarious charity. Brother Saffery was the reverse of all this ; He arrived in a post chaise, and was a tall man of a florid complexion, and very great diameter. Nevertheless it was easy to see that his was no common character. His brow was knit together very gloomily—and his voice (naturally a deep-toned bass) was compressed into an inharmonious whine,—all denoting profound humility and passive obedience. He spoke of the designs of Providence and the projects of the Devil with great *sang-froid;* and quoted largely from the Scripture, backing his quotations with Wiltshire proverbs—and other baser stuff of his own composition. His conversation, you will easily believe then, was very oppressive. Indeed, so strongly did it savour of stupidity, if not of something worse, that I could not perceive it to be at all a pressing duty to put money into the hands of persons like him, for any purpose whatever. However, Brother Saffery had no great room for misguiding the talent committed to his care by the people of Annan;—inasmuch as said talent amounted only to two pounds four shillings and sixpence—a sum which, considering the trouble he put himself to, was trifling enough. It is pity that the missionaries cant so violently.— There is no doubt that many of them are serious, well-meaning men—yet it would be too much to expect that, in such a number, there should not be several with whom the propagation of Christianity is far from being the primary object; and of the best it is to be regretted that their zeal is not tempered by a little more prudence.

I had several other matters to write about; but my paper draws to a close. Yet I cannot forbear noticing that strange project of going to France, which you talk of. Possibly it might be extremely pleasant,—but there are many perplexing questions to be answered before it can be put in execution. First, how are we to get to France; second, how are we to live in France; and third, what good will living in France do to us. "Chill penury," my dear Mitchell, here as in other cases, represses our "noble rage" of visiting this country, and, may be, it is no great matter. For it may be doubted, one would think, whether a country inhabited by fierce revolutionists, and rascally marauders, and flimsy aristocrats—all sweating under a foreign and arbitrary yoke—would be a fit place for an honest man to dwell in—if he could help it. At any rate, it seems I am to stay nearer home for a while. For, you must know, I have received two letters from Professor Christison concerning the situation of Teacher to the Parish School of Kirkcaldy—or rather, I believe, assistant to the present teacher, who (being a very useless man) has agreed to resign upon consideration of being allowed to retain his salary—retaining also the name without any of the power of Parish Schoolmaster. I cannot say that I am violently taken with this offer. The emolument is rated about a hundred-a-year, but there appear to be some ambiguities about it which I do not understand ; and I have written to them, that if they should like to wait, I could come to Edinburgh in Autumn, and talk with them about the place—and if they should not like to wait, that there would be an end of the matter. And there it stands. I wish you would send me as long a letter as this by this day week—I wish also that you would come down and see me—say on a Saturday when the tide is about mid-day, and then we might cross the water to Skinburness. Write soon—send me West's *Exercise*, that I mentioned last time — and believe me, dear Mitchell, yours ever,   THOMAS CARLYLE.

The project referred to in the preceding letter of leaving Annan and becoming master of the school at Kirkcaldy took effect. Carlyle in his *Reminiscences*, i. 98 *sqq.*, gives an account of the circumstances of this change. Its first great result was the making friendship with Edward Irving. " Blessed conquest of a Friend in this world ! That was mainly all the wealth I had for five or six years coming, and it made my life in Kirkcaldy (*i.e.* till near 1819, I think) a happy season in comparison, and a genially useful. Youth itself—healthy, well-intending youth—is so full ·of opulences! I always rather like Kirkcaldy to this day. Annan the reverse rather still when its *gueuseries* come into my head, and my solitary quasi-enchanted position among them,—unpermitted to kick them into the sea."

XIII.—To Mr. ROBERT MITCHELL, Ruthwell Manse.

ANNAN, 3*d August* 1816.

MY DEAR LAD—You will easily guess, by the speediness with which I have answered your letter, that I am anxious to be reinstated in your favour. We have indeed written to one another much too seldom of late. I suppose a good part of the blame is my own —but I will not take it all. Let us try to be more regular in future. I was at a loss what to make of the first part of your letter. I could have laughed at the causes which your sagacity has pointed out for the mistake, had I not been grieved at the mistake itself. You expect my explanation, but in truth I am unable to give any explanation of the matter. I am altogether unconscious of having mentioned any particular Saturday for our excursion; and had I done so, I cannot conceive how I should have hit on that day you speak of, for I must have known that the tide would not serve. If you have not destroyed that letter, I think you will find in it that I wished you to come on the first Saturday that would suit our purpose. But in. reality it was late at night, or rather early in the morning, before I finished that ·immense epistle,—and I dare say I was half asleep over the latter part of it; and so I cannot vouch for its contents. But let us be of comfort. I have looked into the *Belfast Town and Country Almanack*— and consulted several cunning men on the subject,—and from all quarters I collect that the moon will be full about one of the clock on the morning of Thursday the 8th inst.—so that in all human probability—the time of full sea, next Saturday after that, will be between 1 and 2 o'clock;—a time that will answer our purpose very well. Now, if notwithstanding your late disappointment you could be induced to come to Annan about twelve o'clock that day—we could eat a morsel

of dinner together—and forthwith embark for
Cumberland. I am anxious that you should
come—for I wish to see you; and this will be
a pleasant enough way of spending the time;
and besides it will do no harm to you—it may
happen to be of service. Write on Tuesday if
you can; and at any rate on Thursday, and let
me know if you can come. . . . .

I am very glad that you have met with a
book of Natural Philosophy that you like.
Send me your demonstration (or bring it) of
the accelerated motion. I return always to the
study of Physics with more pleasure after trying
the " Philosophy of Mind!" It is delightful,
after wandering in the thick darkness of metaphysics, to behold again the fair face of truth.
When *will* there arise a man who will do for
the science of Mind what Newton did for that
of Matter—establish its fundamental laws on the
firm basis of induction—and discard for ever
those absurd theories that so many dreamers
have devised? I believe this is a foolish question,—for its answer is—never. I am led to
talk in this manner by having lately read

Stewart's *History of Philosophy* in the Supplement to the *Encyclopædia Britannica.* I doubt
I am going to displease you—but I must say—
that I do not recollect of ever having bestowed
as much attention with so little effect upon
any author as upon Professor Stewart. Let
me study his writings as I like, my mind seems
only to turn on its axis,—but without progress-
ive or retrograde motion at all. During these
eighteen months, for example, have I been at
times labouring to comprehend the difference
between the *primary and secondary qualities*
of bodies, and my labour has always been in
vain. Can you resolve me this difficulty? I
can easily see that *heat* (a secondary quality)
has two meanings,—either it means the sensation in our mind—or it means the disposition
of the particles of the body that causes this
sensation : but is not hardness (and the other
primary qualities) in the same predicament?

I designed to say many other things—but
Post-John is about to set out—and I must hold
my hand. Write me at the time I mentioned
—and see if you can come at the time speci-

fied. I have many things to show you and tell you—and ask you. I remain, in the meantime (in great haste), my dear friend, yours truly,

THOMAS CARLYLE.

XIV.—To Mr. R. MITCHELL, Ruthwell Manse.

MAINHILL,[1] 13*th November* 1816.

MY DEAR MITCHELL—I shall set out for Edinburgh to-morrow morning ; and before going, I have begun (as in duty bound) to give you an account of my procedure. I have done nothing at all since I saw you, but put off my time. I was sick two or three days ; and went over to Allonby to recreate myself. I returned from Allonby in three days, and remained

---

[1] " He " [my Father] " became Farmer (of a wet clayey spot called Mainhill) in 1815, that so ' he might keep all his family about him,' struggled with his old valour, and here too prevailed."—*Reminiscences*, i. 61. " About two miles distant " from Ecclefechan, " on the left hand side as you go towards Lockerby, there stands, about three hundred yards in from the road, a solitary low whitewashed cottage, with a few poor out-buildings attached to it. This is Mainhill, which was now for many years to be Carlyle's *home*. . . . The situation is high, utterly bleak, and swept by all the winds. . . . The view alone redeems the dreariness of the situation."—Froude, *Life*, i. p. 35.

mostly at home, waiting with patience for the
day of my departure, which at length is near
at hand.

I am glad you got on so well with your
mathematics. Your demonstration of that
theorem of West—about the triangle—which
you sent me, is very simple and neat, much
better than mine, as far as I can recollect. . . .
I have got nothing to send you—of any use—
unless you think of inserting[1] the following
problem; which notwithstanding the technical
jargon, with which it is enveloped, is after all
a silly enough piece of work. You will perceive that it is a general solution of the
problem, concerning a particular case, of which
Mr. White was so facetious above two years
ago. It is almost the only thing I have done
since I saw you : and as I now write it out for
the first time, I am not without apprehensions
of errors in the computation, though sure enough
of the principle. But if you propose it, I shall
have time enough to give it a revisal before a
solution is required. . . . .

1 *Viz.*, in the *Dumfries Courier*, Mr. Duncan's newspaper.

But here is Johnstone with intelligence that my intended *compagnon de voyage* cannot go to-morrow; and I must off in the coach to-night at six o'clock. " Night thickens, and the crow makes wing to the rooky wood." I have not a moment to lose. Good-bye, my dear Mitchell. You shall hear of me ere long.— Yours ever,

THOMAS CARLYLE.

XV.—To Mr. ROBERT MITCHELL, Ruthwell Manse.

KIRKCALDY, 12*th February* 1817.

MY DEAR SIR—I yesterday received a letter from our friend Johnstone, who tells me that you are greatly astonished at my long silence. And in truth you have some reason, but you are wide of the mark in the hypothesis which you have formed to account for the phenomenon. I am certainly much dissatisfied with your conduct ; but this could only have induced me to write with greater vehemence and celerity. The truth is, I began you a letter about three weeks after my arrival in this place, and had proceeded a great way—when some stupid

business or other interrupted me; and the paper
was thrown by for ten days. I began another
with renovated zeal, and had actually got to the
last page, when your letter from Edinburgh
arrived—and struck me dumb with grief and
surprise. I was in a sad taking. To think
that my very last employment before leaving
home was writing to you—that I had calculated
the weeks and days that must elapse before
the month of March could bring us together
to hold a solemn conference touching all that
should concern us; and then to hear in the
midst of my calculations, that though during a
fortnight you were within ten miles of me—
that though in two hours from any given point
of time you might have been transported to
my habitation—you came not near me! It
was a dog's trick, Mitchell. Little prevented
me from throwing down my implements and
crossing the salt sea to seek you,—had I
known to what quarter of the great city my
search must be directed. All that remained
for me then, was, by writing a most abusive
letter, to show you how much "the galled jade—

will wince." But alas! no sooner had I collected my energies for this enterprise, than a
sore throat seized me—and (after a protracted
struggle on my part) confined me nearly a
whole week to my room. My heart died within me at the sight of the gargles and boluses
and blisters with which I was assailed : and till
two days ago, I was able to think of nothing
but the sickness and sorrow to which mortal
man is subject in this miserable planet. This
is the reason of my silence. You will perceive
that the blame rests with you and fortune. I
am faultless—or nearly so. Still I am in a
very considerable rage against you. Whether
"mine anger shall abate" upon consideration
of a long letter speedily sent me, I know not—
but I wish you would make the experiment.
Johnstone will have told you all about my condition and operations in this long and dirty
town ; and it would but fatigue you to repeat
the statement. I am sufficiently comfortable ;
and feel considerably less spleen and ennui
than I used to do at Annan. My habits have
been so much deranged by change of place,

that I have not yet got rightly settled to my studies.

I have read little since I saw you ; and of that little I doubt I have not made the best use. Have you seen Playfair's Introductory Essay in the *Encyclopædia*? I am sure you will like it. It is distinguished for its elegance and perspicuity. I perused it some weeks ago, and thought it greatly preferable to Stewart's. Indeed, I have often told you that I am somewhat displeased with myself because I cannot admire this great philosopher half as much as many critics do. He is so very stately—so transcendental, and withal so unintelligible, that I cannot look upon him with the needful veneration. I was reading the second volume of his *Philosophy of the Human Mind* lately. It is principally devoted to the consideration of Reason. The greater part of the book is taken up with statements of the opinions of others ; and it often required all my penetration to discover what the Author's own views of the matter were. He talks much about Analysis and Mathematics, and disports him very pleasantly upon geometrical reasoning; but leaves what is to me the principal difficulty untouched. Tell me if you have read it. You have no doubt seen the *Tales of my Landlord.* Certainly, *Waverley* and *Mannering* and the *Black Dwarf* were never written by the same person. If I mistake not, Dr. M'Crie's strictures are a little too severe on some occasions, —and his love of the Cameronians too violent. The worthy Doctor's humour is as heavy as lead. I am afraid you are tired of this.

It is very comfortable that you and Samuel Cowan go on so lovingly together. I am unacquainted with your lucubrations; for I have not seen a *Courier* since I left Dumfriesshire. Long ago, when I was in Edinburgh, I had demonstrated a theorem for your behoof—but I have nearly forgot it now. I think it may be enunciated thus: " If the diameter of a circle be divided internally and externally in the same ratio, the straight lines drawn from one of the points of section to the extremities of the chord passing through the other, will make equal angles with that diameter." It bears some analogy to one of Mathew Stewart's. You will get the demonstration well enough. Johnstone tells me that Mr. Duncan has engaged a certain Mr. M'Diarmid to assist him in conducting the paper. I think I have heard of this person's speeches in the forum— and also that his wit was very great. I hope in his hand the torch of eloquence will burn bright—and shed a strong ray of intellectual light over the whole district.

I have not been in Edinburgh since you left it ; and therefore I can give little news from that quarter. Your countryman Frank Dixon came into the town a few days ago ; and I believe he intends to remain, if he can obtain employment.[1] He was in this place last week, visiting Edward Irving. He is a fellow of infinite jest, and spares no pains to keep his company in convulsions. A variety of works

---

[1] The readers of Carlyle's *Reminiscences* will recall the figure of this "Annandale Rabelais," "a notable kind of man, and one of the memorabilities ;" "a most quizzing, merry, entertaining, guileless, and unmalicious man ; with very considerable logic, reading, contemptuous observation, and intelligence, much real tenderness too," etc. etc.—i. 145.

have been begun about the new year (as is the fashion) in the " periodical line." A weekly newspaper, the *Scotsman*, has reached the third number. I have seen them all —a little violent in their Whiggism; but well enough written in some places. Pillans and Jeffrey and Moncrieff and many others have been respectively named as the Editor. There is also a weekly essay, *The Sale Room*, begun about six weeks ago—by whom, I know not. The writers are not without abilities; but the last numbers seemed to indicate that the work was about to give up the ghost. I understand you had the famous Dr. Spurzheim [1] among you lately, examining the head of George Ross. What said the sage cranioscopist about this wonderful being ? And what do you think of his doctrine of skulls ? For myself—having never been within the sphere of his influence,

---

[1] Spurzheim, originally a disciple of Gall, had come to England in 1813, when he was thirty-seven years old, full of enthusiasm to propagate his new doctrine of phrenology. He was received with especial favour in Scotland, and gained a large following there—among those whose heads were not as hard as Carlyle's.

there is little merit in being sceptical. I own his system seems to me to be a mass of crude hypotheses with a vile show of induction about it—calculated to impose only upon the lazy and wonder-loving. I say *show* of induction, for it seems from the nature of the case to require a number of experiments almost immense to establish any one of its positions. There are, it seems, three-and-thirty bumps upon the human headpiece, which the Doctor says are faculties. Now, any peculiar character may have originated from one of these, or from two or more of them, or from the whole together. Calculate the combinations that can be made of thirty-three bumps, and allow for the original constitution of the mind, and you will require, I believe, millions of instances to prove the title of one single bump to the name of organ. Tell me what you think of this.

I am very much afraid that you will think this letter dull—I think it so myself—but what can I help it? Be as content with it as you can. I am longing greatly to hear from you. Let me know all that you are reading and saying and thinking. Stand not upon ceremony, but send me a very long close-written letter, with all the speed imaginable. Remember me kindly to Mr. and Mrs. Duncan, and to all about the Manse that care for me. Write soon. Good-night, my old friend; I am in a hurry, for the post hour is nearly come.

Thomas Carlyle.

XVI.—To Mr. Robert Mitchell, Ruthwell Manse.

Kirkcaldy, 31*st March* 1817.

My dear Mitchell—Certainly your letter ought to have been answered before this. But it seems to be the fate of all my lucubrations to be behind their time. I have no excuse to offer, except, of course, no time and no subject,—and I need not aggravate my offence by taking up your time longer with discussing it. If you shall be graciously pleased to pardon me, I promise to behave in future as becometh me. I have nothing surprising to tell you. I myself am leading a quiet and peaceable life; and my neighbours, like every other person's neighbours, are exclaiming against the hardness of the times, and praising or blaming the proceedings of the Government, according as the late "strengthening of the hands of the Executive" happens to strike their mental optics. We had two lectures upon the pathognomy of Drs. Gall and Spurzheim lately. The cranioscopist was a Mr. Allen, a Yorkshire man, who has been expounding the doctrines of "chemical philosophy" amongst us for the last three months. He seems to possess talents,—but to be very much addicted to building hypotheses. On this occasion he had the honour of addressing all that was rich and fair and learned in the burgh. After considerable flourishing, he ventured to produce this child of the Doctor's brain—and truly it seemed a very Sooterkin.[1] I have since looked into the Doctor's book,— and if possible the case is worse. Certainly it is not true that our intellectual and moral

[1] " It is reported of the Dutch women that making so great a use of stoves, and often putting them under their petticoats, they engender a kind of ugly monster which is called a *sooterkin*."—Note to *Hudibras*, part iii. canto ii. 146.—T. C.

and physical powers are jumbled in such huge
disorder; surely it will be marvellous if these
powers can be defined and estimated with such
mathematical precision from the size and figure
of the skull.   It is very silly to say that
Spurzheim has *demonstrated* all this; Spurzheim has demonstrated nothing.   For anything
he knows to the contrary, the faculties of the
soul are to be ascertained by the figure and
size of the abdomen—if the venerable science
of Palmistry is not to be revived.   It is in
vain to rail against the opposition shown to
novelties; the doctrine is not to be rejected
for its novelty, but for its want of truth.
Neither does it serve any purpose to tell us
of the many ingenious persons who support it.
A century has not elapsed since Dr. Berkeley
wrote a book on the virtues of Tar-water,
and the learned in Europe were loud in its
praise: yet now tar-water is accounted vile.
So it may fare with Spurzheim.   Nevertheless
Allen has converted the lieges of Kirkcaldy.
So strong is the desire which we all feel of
knowing the character, talents, and disposition

of our neighbour, and so deep is the regret, that

> "Nature has made his breast no windores   ——
> To publish what he does within doors, etc.,"

that (to say nothing of other inducements) craniology, if urged with a proper quantity of dogmatism, will find many believers. And why not ? *Si populus vult decipi, decipiatur.*   ⌐

I was in Edinburgh two weeks ago; but there was nothing worthy of notice taking place. I heard Leslie give a lecture on Heat : it displayed great ingenuity, but his experiments did not succeed. His Geometry is to be out in a few days. I intended to have enrolled in the Divinity Hall; but their Doctor was too busily engaged otherwise to attend to me.[1] He had been quarrelling with his

[1] "Irving's visits and mine to Edinburgh were mostly together, and had always their attraction for us in the meeting with old acquaintances and objects of interest, but except from the books procured could not be accounted of importance. . . . On one of those visits my last feeble tatter of connection with Divinity Hall affairs or clerical outlooks was allowed to snap itself and fall definitely to the ground. Old Dr. Ritchie 'not at home' when I called to enter myself. 'Good,' answered I ; 'let the omen be fulfilled.'"—*Reminiscences*, i. 115.

students about the management of the library; and the committee, which has been appointed to draw up regulations for the management of it, had that very day submitted them to the Doctor and his students assembled in the Hall. They gave much dissatisfaction to the Doctor, and immediately (as I was told—for I was not there) there was great confusion, and several speeches, vituperative and objurgatory, passed among them; till at last the mutineers, to the number of fifty, adjourned to a neighbouring schoolroom, *con strepitu*, and valiantly drew up twelve resolutions proclaiming their grievances, and their determination to apply to the Presbytery for advice. The Senatus Academicus has since taken up the case; and, as the committee appointed to decide on it consists of Meiklejohn, Ritchie and Brunton, it is easy to see how the affair will end. Your picture of this Hall, and the dudgeon it seems to have excited in you, gave me great amusement. I have not been within its walls for many months —and I know not whether I shall ever return, but all accounts agree in representing it as

one of the most melancholy and unprofitable
corporations that has appeared in these parts
for a great while. If we are to judge of the
kind of Professors we should get from the
Edinburgh Kirk by the sample we already
possess, it is devoutly to be wished that their
visits may be short and far between. It may
safely be asserted that though the Doctors
Ritchie, junior and senior, with Dr. Meiklejohn, Dr. Brunton, and Dr. Brown, were to
continue in their chairs, dozing, in their present
fashion, for a century, all the knowledge which
they could discover would be an imperceptible
quantity—if indeed its sign were not negative.
We ought to be somewhat sorry for the—
Divinity Hall; but our grief need not stop
here. If we follow its members into the world,
and observe their destination, we shall find it
very pitiful. With the exception of the few
whom superior talents or better stars exempt
from the common fortune, every Scotch Licentiate must adopt one of two alternatives. If
he is made of pliant stuff he selects some one
having authority, before whom he bows with

unabating alacrity for (say) half a score of
years, and thereby obtains a Kirk, whereupon
he betakes him to collect his stipend, and
(unless he think of persecuting the Schoolmaster) generally in a few months falls into a
state of torpor, from which he rises no more.
If, on the other hand, the soul of the Licentiate
is stubborn, and delights not to honour the
Esquires of the district;—heartless and hope-
less he must drag out his life—without aim or
object—vexed at every step to see surplices
alighting on the backs of many who surpass
him in nothing but their *love for gravy*.[1] This
is the result of patronage, and this is one of
the stages through which every established
Church must pass, in its road to dissolution.
No government ever fostered a Church un- —
less for its value as a State-engine, and none
was ever ignorant of the insecurity of this
engine till it is placed upon the rock of
patronage. But it ends not here. Though

[1] " I would advise every young man " (says Dr. Goldsmith),
"at his entrance into the world, *to like gravy:* I was once
disinherited by an old Uncle for not liking gravy " (from
memory).—T. C.

all "constituted authorities" are ready to admit that Truth is great and will prevail—none have ventured to let their "true religion" descend unsupported into the arena, and try its hand at mauling the heresies which oppose it. On the contrary, every "true religion" is propped— and bolstered, and the hands of its rivals tied up ; till by nursing and fattening it has become a bloated monster that human nature can no longer look upon—and men rise up and knock its brains out. Then there is great joy for a season, and forthwith a successor is elected, which undergoes the same treatment—and in process of time meets with a similar fate. Such is the destiny of Churches by law established. Let every one of us be as contented with it as possible—and gird up his loins to attain unto a share of the plate, whilst the game is good.

I am glad that you like Adam Smith. I agree with you very cordially, and regard him as one of the most honest and ingenious men of his age, or indeed of any other. He is one of the very few writers who have not gone delirious when they came to treat of Metaphysics. He wrote his *Wealth of Nations* in a room not a hundred yards from the place where I am sitting—and the men of Kirkcaldy are with reason proud to remember him. You view Lord Bacon with a different eye; and, without doubt, you have some reason to be scandalised at the admiration with which he is treated. It looks as if philosophers could not do without some one to worship. It is not long since they tumbled poor Aristotle from his temple—and it rests not with Playfair and Stewart, or Bacon would soon be exalted in his stead. I have read little of any consequence since I wrote to you. You will have seen the last numbers of the *Edinburgh* and *Quarterly Reviews.* In the latter, among a great deal of foul and nauseating stuff, I was happy to see that due credit is at last given to Mr. Duncan for his valuable institution.[1] I was reading Pascal's *Lettres*

---

[1] Mr. Henry Duncan, the minister of Ruthwell, near Dumfries (born 1774, died 1846), to whose sons Mitchell was tutor, was a man of good sense and public spirit. He had established at Ruthwell "a Parish Bank for the Savings of the Industrious" (the parent of all modern Savings Banks);

Provinciales.   None can help admiring his wit
and probity.   He sustains excellently the character of *naiveté* which he has assumed—and with
infinite dexterity hunts the Jesuits through all
their doublings and subterfuges, till he has
triumphantly exposed the wretched baseness of
their conduct.   It is pity that the Salvation of
Europe required the re-establishment of this
vile order of men.   Last week I perused Von
Buch's *Travels in Norway and Lapland.*   Much
of his attention is devoted to Mineralogy, of
which I am very ignorant, and his movements
are sometimes not a little mysterious, from the
want of a proper map of the country.   Nevertheless he communicates some valuable information respecting the natural productions and the
wandering inhabitants of those dreary regions.
His manner is as clumsy and ponderous as that
of German philosophers generally is, and nowhere is this more apparent than when he
attempts to be striking, or tries his powers in
the pathetic line.   I took Bailly's *Histoire—*

and he had lately published an account of it, which was noticed
with warm praise in the *Quarterly Review* for January 1817.

de l'Astronomie out of the College library last time I was over the Firth. [He seems] to write with great eloquence and perspicuity; but I have read little of him. We get a *Dumfries Courier* here amongst us. Our third number reached us a few days ago. It seems M'Diarmid is become sole Editor—it is not the opinion of the readers here that the paper has been a gainer by the change. The Ranger seems (under favour) to be but a silly kind of person—and his friend Mr. Bright is a very vapid gentleman. It is a pity that Spondastes[1] his labours have been curtailed before he has completed his investigations. But we must make a shift to live without knowing who wrote *Mary's Dream.* I expected to have seen Samuel Cowan's investigation last week—but it did not appear. If you have given over your Mathematics, well and good; but if you have

---

[1] "Little Murray," wrote Mitchell, 23d February 1817, meaning their common friend Thomas Murray, "has been writing in the *Courier* under the name of *Spondastes.* He gave an account of all the learned Gallovidians from the Creation of the World to the present day; and had not sheer modesty prevented him, himself would have been among the number."

not, you may throw the following exercises into your storeroom, if you like. [Here followed mathematical propositions.]

And now, my beloved Mitchell, what more can I do for thee? My sheet is full—and if thou speak of *pica*[1]—this is dense enough in all conscience. I do hope and trust I shall hear from thee very soon. I know I have been to blame—but that is past and gone. Therefore let us forget and forgive—and believe me, my dear Robin, yours faithfully,

THOMAS CARLYLE.

XVII.—To Mr. R. MITCHELL, Ruthwell Manse.

KIRKCALDY, 5*th July* 1817.

MY DEAR ROBIN—After waiting very impatiently for such a long period, I received with great satisfaction, the short but savoury morsel which thou hast at length been pleased

[1] In the letter to which this is an answer Mitchell had written: "I have selected the largest sheet of paper I have in the world; my 'page' is sufficiently 'dense,' and my type a perfect *pica*,—all this that 'thine anger may abate.' What can I do more?"

to despatch me. It does not by any means quell my appetite; but you assure me it is only a precursor, and what can I do but be " propitiated." I turned pale when I noticed your charge of "palming." The proposition about the harmonic section was, as I said before, included in one of Matthew Stewart's problems, —the source, I suppose, from which Leslie himself obtained it. No doubt it was stupid enough not to know that it was deducible from Prop. 22, iii. of the *Analysis*, or still more directly from prop. 9, vi. *Elements*—and therein lies my error. The problem concerning the minimum was proposed last winter in Leslie's class; and I know not when or where or in what manner you and Waugh had discussed it. That "to find the locus of the vertex of a triangle given in species whose base is one of the sides of a given angle standing on a given straight line," was also derived from one of Leslie's. It seems to have no affinity with prop. 4, iii. *Analysis*. I suppose it has been wrongly enunciated to you. So that you see the quantity of palming has in this case been very inconsiderable. The same day on which I received your letter, I perused Alpha's Newspaper-solution. Edward Irving thinks it a learned investigation. I think so likewise. The very same result (for I tried it) is obtained, and by a nearly similar process, from the 32d prop. of Newton : but I do not understand your integral calculus. It would be a more difficult business to find the time of descent to the centre of the earth. I wish you would try this and send me your result. I am afraid I cannot do it.

Three weeks ago I finished M. Bailly's *His-toire de l'Astronomie Moderne.* His acquaintance with the science seems to have been more extensive than profound ; his style is elegant — perhaps too florid, and interspersed with metaphors which an English critic might be tempted sometimes to call conceited. I wish I were an Astronomer. Is it not an interesting reflection to consider, that a little creature such as man—though his eye can see the heaven but as it were for a moment—is able to delineate the aspect which it presented long ages before

he came into being—and to predict the aspects
which it *will* present when ages shall have
gone by ?   The past, the present, and the
future are before him.   Assuredly the human
species never performed a more honourable
achievement.   " The boast of heraldry, the
pomp of power," must disappear like those that
delighted in them ; but when the hand that
wrote the *Principia* is reduced to a little black
earth, and the spirit that dictated it is gone no
one knows whither—the work itself remains in
undecaying majesty to all generations.   But
Dr. Chalmers, it would seem, is fearful lest
these speculations lead us away from Christianity, and has written a volume of *Discourses*
to prove that the insignificance of our planet in
the Universe is no argument against the truth
of religion.   Orthodox men declare, of course,
that he has completely discomfited his oppon-
ents.   I read it some time ago.   It abounds in
that fiery, thoroughgoing style of writing for
which the Author is so remarkable ; nevertheless his best argument seems to be, that as it is
in the Scriptures, we have no business to think

about it at all—an argument which was well
enough known to be a panacea in cases of that
nature before his volume saw the light. One
is a little surprised to see the Doctor so
vehement in his praise of Newton for what
certainly was very laudable—his rejecting all
manner of probabilities, and refusing to admit
any hypothesis till it was supported by direct
and uncontrovertible proof. Without doubt
this answers exactly in the present instance,
but if carried to its full extent on the other side,
it will lead to alarming results. Christianity
itself is only supported by probabilities; very
strong ones certainly, but still only probabilities.
But here, we are informed, it is necessary "to
sit down with the docility of little children"
and believe everything that is told us; which
is a very comfortable way of reasoning. It is
perhaps not surprising that the Author should
be dogmatical; but it seems strange, when his
own side of the question is so very evident,
that he should deal so largely in denunciations
against his adversaries. It is very certain that
the unhappy sceptic cannot believe one jot the

better, though he were brayed in a mortar.
Yet almost all the writers on the evidences of
Christianity that I have seen (excepting Paley)⌐
have treated him in this manner. These reflections occur naturally enough in perusing
this book (which after all is no ordinary production, though better books have not always
passed through six editions in so short a space);
but I have not stated them often. When a⌐
poor creature's sentiments, in such cases, happen to be contrary to those of his neighbours,
the less he says of them the better. This ⌐
same Doctor, as you will know, writes the first
article in the late *Edinburgh Review*—on the
"Causes and Cure of Mendicity." After ex-
patiating at considerable length upon the evils
of pauperism, he proposes, as a remedy, to
increase the number of clergymen. They who
know the general habits of Scottish ministers
will easily see how sovereign a specific this is.
The remainder of the *Review* is good reading;
but as you will have seen it before this time, I
will not trouble you further on the matter. I
have seen the last Number of the *Quarterly*⌐

Review. It seems to be getting into a very
rotten frothy vein. Mr. Southey is a most
unblushing character ; and his political lucubrations are very notable. He has been sorely
galled by the Caledonian oracle, poor man. I
know nothing about Mr. Duncan's controversy
except through the *Scotsman;* and they assign
him the victory. I received about a month
ago the Rev. William Thomson of Ochiltree's
new translation of the Testament. Of course
I am no judge of his " new renderings ;" but
the style, both of writing and thinking, displayed in those parts which I have looked at,
is dull and sluggish as the clay itself. He
brags of having altered the expressions of the
old translation — everybody, I suppose, will
readily admit this, and be ready to wish him
joy of all the honours that can arise from
such alterations. I might say more of books,
but this will abundantly satisfy you for one
course.

I have heard nothing of Johnstone yet.
Truly, I think, never any poor wight had
two such lazy correspondents as I am yoked

withal. Much might be said on this subject—
but it is needless to punish you before the time.
In four or five weeks I hope to be with you, and
you shall hear your evil deeds [proclaimed] with
energy enough. As I may reach Annandale
by various routes, it will be an object of great
importance to fix upon the best. Sometimes
I am for proceeding through Peebles and the
wolds of Selkirk by Polmoodie and Ettrick
Pen. This track is almost as the crow flies.
At other times I think of Tweedsmuir and
Moffat; and at present Irving and a Mr.
Pears (schoolmaster in this neighbourhood)
are persuading me to accompany them by
Stirling and the Trossachs to Glasgow.[1] They
tell me we shall see Loch Katrine and climb
Ben Lomond and do many other exploits;—
but we have not yet counted the cost—and
notwithstanding all that has been said about
the sturdy independent feelings of a pedestrian,
I am inclined to think that in my case they
are greatly overbalanced by the more vulgar

[1] Of this journey there is a lively account in the *Reminiscences*, i. 122-134.

consideration of stiffened joints and blistered feet. Upon the whole it is not unlikely that I must again penetrate the moors of Tweeddale —a district which I never crossed except in the most woful plight both of body and mind— and which therefore I hate very cordially. At all events, I am to be three or four weeks beside you. I wish you would contrive some excursion for our mutual benefit. What say you of a sail to Liverpool? The expense would not be great—and it might tend to dissipate that headache which, I am sorry to find, still infests you. We could embark at Dumfries or Annan, and we could not fail to find a ship bound to some Scottish port when-ever it should please us to return. We could go to the Isle of Man or to Wigtown or any-whither. If Johnstone would go with us, we should be three merry souls—wind and weather permitting. Write me your opinion of this project immediately—I had other things to tell you of—but daylight and paper are both failing me,—and this half-hour I have been driving my pen as fast as ever Jehu, the son of Nimshi,—

drove his chariot, to be in time for the mail,—
and, after all, I am afraid that I am out. One
thing I must mention. Write soon; call to
mind thy engagements, and, to make the
matter definite, I hereby give you notice that
unless I receive a letter from thee within
fourteen days from the date hereof (allowing
three days of grace) thou shalt be punished as
a *crack tryst*[1] and a breaker of promise, without
benefit of clergy—so look to it. Thine old and
faithful friend,
                                    THOMAS CARLYLE.

XVIII.—To Mr. JAMES JOHNSTONE, Hitchill,[2] Annan.

KIRKCALDY, 25*th September* 1817.

MY DEAR JOHNSTONE—I fear you are already
fretting at my silence; and, as I have no satisfactory apology to offer, it would but augment your
dudgeon to attempt one. Therefore, without
preface, I desire you to be content, and you
shall hear all things in their order. To begin

---

[1] One who does not fulfil his engagement.
[2] Hitchill, a substantial farmhouse, built by Carlyle's
father, stands about midway between Ruthwell and Annan.
Johnstone was tutor to Mr. Church's sons there.

at the beginning—the day after my parting with
you and Mitchell was rainy, and I spent it at
home in a state of torpid and unprofitable dreaming. But next morning being dry, I resolved
to commence my journey. Sandy accompanied
me to Moffat; and during my ride my mind
was occupied with all the cheering reflections
which a passage through Tweedsmuir, the re-
commencement of Paedagogy, and the jolting of
a strong cart-horse naturally inspired. About
two o'clock I was on the summit of Ericstane. I looked down through the long deep
vale of the Annan, remembered my friends
upon the dim horizon, and half-uttering the wish
that rose within me for their welfare, I turned
me round and pursued the tenor of my way.
In a short time I overtook two fellow travellers.
One of them was a peasant of those parts : the
other a stout square-made [man] of thirty in
sailor's clothes, without shoes or shirt, with a
countenance that seemed tanned by wind and
weather, and expressive at once of energy and
harmlessness. Upon investigation, I found that
this unlucky person was one Thomas Cuvallo,

a native of Constantinople, whose father had
gone from the neighbourhood of Corinth—that
he had served two years on board the Achilles
English ship of war—was discharged in 1814
—had afterwards been twice at India, whence
he had returned last spring—and that travelling
from one harbour to another in the vain hope
of finding a vessel to carry him to his own
country, he had expended all his money, and
was now, as a last resort, making his way to
Leith to try to procure either a passage to the
Continent, or work to keep him from starving
till times should mend. This Thomas Cuvallo,
cast thus forlornly upon the wolds of Tweeddale,
seemed to view his condition with an indifference that Zeno himself might have envied. The
present of a piece of bread and cheese, which
Mrs. Johnston had stowed into my pocket at
Moffat, secured me his favour, and rendered
him very communicative—though his stock of
English vocables was far from extensive. After
repeating me the Greek alphabet, he gave me
the names of several objects in Romaic—most
of which bore a striking resemblance to the

Hellenic ; and when I inquired the signification of *Zoë mou sas agapo*, he replied with a grin of intelligence—" My life, I love thee." Then he proceeded to unfold to me the various grievances and molestations to which he (being a Djour) was exposed in Istambol—interspersing some account of his adventures in the Levant, together with notices of Mullahs, Jemams, and spinning Dervishes. ·Insensibly he digressed into the subject of magic and divination—and then set about revealing to me his ideas touching miracles and spectres. He said there were ten kinds of spectres. Under the head of miracles, he told me of certain pictures in St. Sophia's Church which no efforts of the Turks can efface, though they scrape and whitewash never so manfully. In the same church, it seems, there is a pulpit into which these unhappy Mussulmans can never gain admittance —axes and crows avail them nothing : but every Easter-eve there appears in it the figure of a man reading in a book, which when he shall have finished, the Mohammedan empire shall pass away for ever. He told me likewise

of a well in Constantinople which contains a
fish whose history is very remarkable. It happened to be frying in a pan in the palace at the
time the Turks were about to enter the city;
when the incredulous and phlegmatic sovereign
declared to the General who came to ask his
advice, that he would as soon believe that this
fish would jump from his frying-pan and live,
as that the Turks were within many leagues
of him. Whereupon the fish sprang out with
great agility, and at this hour, he said, is living
in its well—one side roasted and the other raw
—and intends to do so till Greece shall be
finally delivered from bondage. He never saw
it, but his mother did. On our arrival at the
Bield, I presented this unfortunate Argive with
a draught of porter; and leaving him—with a
shilling, half a foot of tobacco, and my best
wishes—to exert his begging powers in the
neighbourhood, I advanced to Broughton in
the midst of rain, and reached it at nightfall.
In about half an hour there came a *return
chaise*, into which I mounted: and after being
dosed by the quaverings of a foolish Grocer who

frequently attempted to sing, and sometimes amused by the proofs which our driver (a kind of Cuddie Headrigg fellow) produced of the insanity of Kennedy and his fair wife—both of renowned memory in your country, I came to Noblehouse at ten o'clock. Next day at noon I was in Edinburgh ; met with Irving at Leith in the evening, and finally without loss or detriment I reached my habitation in time for tea.

Thus you see, after all the pains and pleasures, and triumphs and discomfitures, and perils by land and water, which a month spent in journeying upon the face of this fair earth has caused me to experience, I find myself once more seated in my little chamber, in this ancient burgh of Kirkcaldy—all my labours (like those of many wiser persons) having brought me only to the place from whence I started. Now that I have shaken hands with my honest neighbours, and resumed my occupations, I find that the remembrance of the wild and wondrous features of the Highlands assorts but awkwardly with the vulgar feelings to which the duties of a school give rise. Nevertheless I am peaceful

and contented, and my days pass on pleasantly enough. What I deplore is that laziness
and dissipation of mind tò which I am still subject. At present I am quieting my conscience
with the thought that I shall study very diligently
this winter. Heaven grant it be so! for without increasing in knowledge what profits it to
live? Yet the commencement has been inaus-
picious. Three weeks ago I began to read
Wallace's *Fluxions* in the *Encyclopædia*, and
had proceeded a little way, when the *Quarterly
Review*, some problems in a very silly *Literary
and Statistical Magazine* of which the Schoolmasters are supporters, Madam de Staël's *Ger-
many*, etc. etc., have suspended my operations
these ten days. After all I am afraid that this
winter will pass as others have done before it
—unmarked by improvement; and what is to
hinder the next, and its followers till the end of
the short season allotted me, to do so likewise?
Pitiful destiny! my friend—yet how to be
avoided? Lately I was renewing my old project of going to the French University. I have
flattered myself with the thought that the colli-

sion with so many foreign minds, all toiling with might and main after the same object, would excite in me a permanent enthusiasm sufficient to carry me as far as my powers would go— straight forward—and not in the zig-zag direc-— tions—now flying, now creeping, which I at present pursue. Once I had almost determined next time I went to Edinburgh to inquire whether it would be possible to put this scheme in execution. But I suppose it will shortly dissipate—like other schemes of a similar nature, and leave me to form resolutions, and lament their failure as before. You will think me very weak and silly : I think so myself (*hinc illae lacrymae*), and know not whether I shall ever mend. I hope you order these matters better at Hitchill.

I told you I had seen the *Quarterly Review.*— You would notice its contents in the newspaper. It is a long time since I ceased to be one of its admirers. The writers possess no inconsiderable share of dogmatism ; and their learning, which they are, to an unpleasant degree, fond of displaying, is of that minute scholastic nature

which is eminently distinguished from knowledge. Moreover their zeal for the "Social
Order" seems to eat them up, and their horror
of revolution is violent as a hydrophobia. These
qualities are prominent in the last number—and
accordingly it contains much disgusting matter;
but I like it better (as a whole) than some of
its predecessors. There is in it a distant and
respectful but severe criticism on Dugald
Stewart's writings, which comes much nearer
my views of his character than any of the
panegyrics which the Edinburgh Reviewers
have so lavishly bestowed upon him. The
other night I sat up till four o'clock reading
Matthew Lewis' *Monk*. It is the most stupid
and villainous novel that I have read for a
great while. Considerable portions of it are
grossly indecent, not to say brutish : one does
not care a straw about one of the characters—
and though "little Mat" has legions of ghosts
and devils at his bidding, one views their
movements with profound indifference. I have
seen the first number of *Constable's Magazine*
—it seems scarcely equal to *Blackwood's*—the

last number of which has appeared. B. advertises a new one with a slight variation in the title. There is also another periodical publication published once a fortnight (I forget its name), begun under the auspices of Peter Hill. I perused only one article and can give no account of it. I cannot pretend to say what this influx of magazines indicates or portends.

Tell Mr. Church that the harvest began here about a week after my arrival. Barley seems to be the principal crop in this neighbourhood— and all hands are now busily engaged in cutting it. It has been sadly tossed and broken by the wind and rain, but as the last fortnight has been excellent weather—the people have great hopes of it yet. What the price of the grain is I know not—new oatmeal was $19\frac{1}{2}$d. the peck— but two days of soft weather have raised it a penny. Make my best compliments to Mrs. Church and Miss Harper. I hope you are happy with them. I long to hear what you are all doing. Write me, I pray you, a full and particular account of all your transactions. Pardon my delays—and let me tell you even now I have been obliged to write this letter most doggedly, and as it were by main force, so great was my desire to keep you in peace. Can you tell me what that knave Mitchell is doing? He should have sent me a letter two weeks ago. Remember me at Bogside. Do write very soon, and believe me, dear Johnstone, yours faithfully,

THOMAS CARLYLE.

P.S.—I am just going down to Irving's to get the newspaper and concert measures for an expedition to Edinburgh, which we are meditating to accomplish to-morrow evening. I shall put this into the office by the way—so good-night once more.

XIX.—To Mr. R. MITCHELL, Ruthwell Manse.

KIRKCALDY, 19*th November* 1817.

It is a great while, my dear Mitchell, since I wrote you a letter that did not require an apology for its lateness. You too are chargeable with similar practices; and could I with any conscience, I would rate you very severely. It

is certainly a deplorable way of proceeding. If
it be true in your case, as it is in mine, that the
letters which pass between us occasion some of
the happiest feelings that diversify this languid
scene—it is pity that they are, on both sides, so
sparingly supplied. I am no stranger to the
dreary sense of vacuity that occupies the soul
of him who sits down to fill a fair unblotted
sheet of paper—when fit materials are wanting.
But we are too fastidious in our choice of
subjects ; and, above all, we ought to exert
ourselves. It cannot be expected, that leading
this unvaried life, which Providence has allotted
us, we should have any wonderful tidings to communicate. We have nothing to say about the
musical glasses, or *bon-ton*, nor can we pretend—
to speak of moving incidents by flood and field,
of Cannibals that each other eat—the Anthro-
pophagi—or aught of that nature. Yet are we
not destitute of topics. The feelings and adventures of each of us (though of no moment
to nearly all the world beside) may be interesting to the other, and by mutually communicating
the progress of our studies, and the ideas (if

any) that at times penetrate these benighted minds of ours—we may be encouraged to proceed on our way; rejoicing together, without flattery or jealousy or any such thing. I desire you to ponder upon this subject with due attention. Let us both write oftener—no matter how dull the letters be. When men cannot be social, they are content to be gregarious—and, though it be in a state of silence and torpor, experience some gratification from mere juxtaposition; so with regard to letters, it may safely be affirmed, that the shortest and meagrest is preferable to none at all. I am writing to you at present from a conviction of the truth and utility of this proposition. Since my departure from your country, nothing at all worth relating has happened to me. I have gone the round of my duties with all the regularity and *sang-froid* of a mill-horse. My mind has on the whole been placid—sometimes almost stagnant. And if it be true, as Flaccus hath it, that

" Nil admirari prope res est una,
  Solaque, quae possit facere et servare beatum,"

I am in a fair way of obtaining and preserving a considerable share of felicity. But I am much inclined to doubt Flaccus. The history of my studies exhibits the same stupid picture of impotent resolutions and unavailing regrets as heretofore. I may lay aside my French project when I please. What, as you say, should take me to Paris?[1] If they could pluck from my brain this rooted indolence, it might be worth thinking of. Soon after my arrival I fell to Wallace's *Fluxions*[2] with might and main. I would study, I thought, with great vehemence, every night—and the two hours at noon which I have to dispose of, I would devote to the reading of history and other lighter matters. But alas! two hours I found to be insufficient —by degrees poor Wallace was encroached upon—and is now all but finally discarded.

[1] "What wild-goose scheme is this of yours of going to France? Do you not know that the Polytechnic School is knocked on the head? The rest are not worth the naming. I say, 'Laddie Dinwoodie o' the Gardenholm, compose yourself to your potatoes there.'" From letter of Mitchell, 4th October 1817.

[2] Wallace was Professor of Mathematics in the University of Edinburgh.

His introduction, it must be confessed, is
ponderous and repulsive.   His horror of the
binomial theorem leads him into strange bye-
paths.   But he demonstrates with great vigour.
The worst of it is, we are led to his conclusion,
as it were through a narrow lane—often, by its
windings shutting from our view the object of
our search, and never affording us a glimpse
of the surrounding country.   I wish I had it
in my head.   But, unless I quit my historical
pursuits, it may be doubted whether this will
ever happen.   I have read through that clear
and candid but cold-hearted narration of David
Hume,—and now seven of Toby Smollett's eight
chaotic volumes are before me.   To say nothing
of Gibbon (of whom I have only read a volume),
nor of the Watsons, the Russells, the Voltaires,
etc. etc., known to me only by name.   Alas!
thou seest how I am beset.   It would be of
little avail to criticise Bacon's *Essays*.   It is
enough to say, that Stewart's opinion of them
is higher than I can attain.   For style, they
are rich and venerable—for thinking, incorrect
and fanciful.   Some time ago I bought me a

copy of La Rochefoucault. It has been said—
that the basis of his system is the supposition
of self-love being the motive of all our actions.
It rather seems as if he had laid down no
system at all. Regarding man as a wretched,
mischievous thing, little better than a kind of
vermin, he represents him as the sport of his
passions, above all of vanity, and exposes the
secret springs of his conduct always with some
wit, and ('bating the usual sacrifices of accuracy
to smartness), in general, with great truth and
sagacity.

I perused your theorems with some attention. They are well worthy of a place in the
Courier—though not for the purpose you mention. Mr. Johnston, if I mistake not, is a small
gentleman, whom it would be no honour to
demolish. I have scarcely done a problem since
I saw you. There is one—"to find the locus
of the vertex of a triangle, whose base is given,
the one angle at the base being double of the
other"—which I was trying some time ago.
You will easily see that the locus is a hyperbola.
The solution of problems, I begin to think,

depends very much upon a certain sleight of hand, that can be acquired without great difficulty by frequent practice. I am not so sure as I used to be that it is the best way of employing oneself. Without doubt it concentrates our Mathematical ideas—and exercises the head; but little knowledge is gained by the process. If I am wrong—put me right when you send me a letter.

It is long since I was at Edinburgh, and when I was there nothing of importance was a doing. I heard Alison[1] preach. His elocution is clear—his style elegant—his ideas distinct rather than profound. Some person contrasting him and Chalmers, observed that the Prebendary of Sarum is like a glass of spruce beer—pure, refreshing, and unsubstantial—the minister of the Tron Kirk, like a draught of Johnnie Dowie's ale,—muddy, thick, and spirit-stirring.

---

[1] The Rev. Archibald Alison, " alors célèbre " as a preacher for the elegance of his style, and as a writer of an " Essay on Taste," which was thought to " deserve a conspicuous place in every well-chosen library." He was a marked figure in the society of Edinburgh.

Ivory[1] the celebrated analyst has quitted his situation at the College of (I forget its name). Wallace has succeeded him—and has left his own place to his brother. They were saying that Ivory had it in his mind to come to Edinburgh, and become a Teacher of Mathematics. Leslie has published an Arithmetic—similar I suppose to that treatise contained in the supplement of the *Encyclopedia.* He is to have a third class this winter. Playfair, I believe, is returned—and is to teach his class himself. Some time since, all the world was astonished at the 2nd number of *Blackwood's* (formerly the *Edinburgh*) *Magazine.* The greater part of it is full of gall : but the most venomous article is the "Translation of a Chaldee Manuscript," said to be found in the Library of Paris. It is written in the phrase of the Scriptures, and [gives] an allegorical account of the origin and end of the late *Edinburgh Magazine* —greatly to the disparagement of Constable

[1] Professor Ivory, born 1765, later Sir James Ivory, gave up in 1819 the chair of Mathematics at the Royal Military College at Sandhurst, which he had held for fifteen years. He succeeded Leslie in the chair of Mathematics in Edinburgh.

and the Editors. Most of the Authors of Edinburgh are characterised with great acrimony—
under the likeness of birds and beasts and
creeping things. Blackwood is like to be be-
leaguered with prosecutions for it—two are
already raised against him. Replies in the
shape of " explanations," " letters to Drs. M 'Crie
and Thomson," have been put forth—more are
promised, and, doubtless, rejoinders are in a
state of preparation. Whatever may become
of Blackwood or his antagonists—the " reading" or rather the talking " public" is greatly
beholden to the Author. He has kept its jaws
moving these four weeks—and the sport is not
finished yet.[1]

As I have nothing more to say, I believe it
will be as well to conclude here, by desiring thee
to commend me to all my friends in thy neighbourhood—and to write immediately if thou
hast any love for—Thine old and trusty friend,

THOMAS CARLYLE.

[1] This " Chaldee Manuscript " was mainly the work of
Hogg, the " Ettrick Shepherd ;" he was assisted by Wilson
and Lockhart. It is reprinted in the collected edition of Pro-

XX.—To Mr. JAMES JOHNSTONE.

KIRKCALDY, 20*th November* 1817.

O thou Turk in grain!—Did not I send thee long ago a letter of three dense pages? Have not I any afternoon these three months turned my eye to the mantelpiece, upon my return from school, to see if peradventure the postman had brought me no word from Hitchill? And did he ever bring me any? Have not I—but what availeth it to talk? In sobriety I am dreadfully enraged. Write me a letter, I say, without further parley, or I will roar (as Bottom saith), so that it shall do any man's heart good to hear me. It is vain to tell me that you have no subject. Send me the meditations of your own heart—send me a register of your domestic occurrences—in short anything—an account of the prices of grain and black cattle rather than nothing at all.

fessor Wilson's works, with notes by his son-in-law, Professor Ferrier. The notoriety it had is due more to the character of the persons referred to in it, and the scandal occasioned by its ill-mannered satire, than to any genuine wit or humour.

My history since I wrote last to you contains
no particular worth relating : I continue to
follow my vocation with a peaceful and quiet
heart, and might live under my vine and fig-
tree, in case I had one, with none to make me
afraid. I will not detain you long with my
studies. I have been reading little except
Coxe's travels in Switzerland, Poland, Russia,
etc., Hume's history, together with part of
Smollett, Gibbon, etc. Coxe is an intelligent
man, and communicates in a very popular
way considerable information concerning the
countries through which he passed. Hume you
know to be distinct and impartial : but he has
less sympathy than might be expected with the
heroic patriots—the Hampdens and the Sid-
neys, that glorify the pages of English history.
I fear Smollett is going to be a confused
creature. I have read but a volume of Gibbon
—and I do not like him : his style is flowery ;
his sarcasms wicked ; his notes oppressive,
often beastly. They that cultivate literary
small-talk have been greatly attracted for some
time by the late number of *Blackwood's* (for-

merly the *Edinburgh*) *Magazine*. It contains
many slanderous insinuations against the pub-
lisher's rivals — particularly a paper entitled
" Translation of a Chaldee Manuscript"—concerning the author and date of which it is
gravely asserted the celebrated Sylvester de
Sacy is writing a dissertation. The piece is
divided into chapters and verses, and written
in the Scripture language. It relates, in an
emblematical manner, the rise, progress, decline
and fall of the late *Edinburgh Magazine*.
Constable and the Editor, as well as most of
the Edinburgh Authors, are bitterly lampooned
—under the similitudes of magicians, enchanters,
spirits, birds, and four-footed beasts. The
writer displays some talent—but his malice
and profanity are as conspicuous as his wit.
Three prosecutions have been raised against
Blackwood on account of it—and the press
is groaning with animadversions and replies. It is curious to observe the importance
which the writings of Walter Scott have
conferred on everything pertaining to the
Border. These manufacturers deal largely in

that article. Not a beldame, in the Merse,[1] can plant her cabbages—nor a tinker solder his kettle, but it must be forthwith communicated to the public in *Blackwood's* or the *Scots Magazine.* As if the Public had anything to do with the matter. I marvel that they have not some correspondent in the West Marches, to transmit them intelligence about the Spoon‑men of Hightae, and the visions of Madam Peel. The dead-lights *"gaun luntin by"*[2] would be a rare morsel for them.

Little occurs in this neighbourhood to disturb our tranquillity—and still less that you would care for hearing. I attended the examination of Irving's Academy lately. He acquitted himself dexterously and seemed to give general satisfaction. His assistant is gone to Edinburgh—and he now manages the school himself—more comfortably, I hear, than formerly. A month ago that same Allen, whom

[1] The Merse or March, one of the divisions of Berwickshire extending from the Lammermoor Hills to the Tweed.

[2] Hightae was the headquarters of the tinkers and spoonmakers in Dumfriesshire. "Madam Peel" of Ecclefechan had a dream, in which she saw the death-lights going fuming by.

I once mentioned before, gave us a concluding lecture on the applications of Spurzheim's theory of Cranioscopy. It was greatly past comprehension. He seemed to have taken the fly-wheels from his brain, and said to it—brain, be at thy speed—produce me stuff—no matter of what colour, shape or texture :—and truly it was a frantic, incoherent story as heart could wish. It appears to have knocked the bottom out of Spurzheim's doctrine in these parts. Next came sundry players and other migratory animals of that sort. Last week we had a reciting man, Mr. Hamilton from Glasgow. Perhaps Miss Harper may have seen him. He understands his trade well; but he is a drinking dog. The other day, there arrived from Edinburgh, a large shoal of preachers— Dixon, Nichol, Bullock, etc.—they preached all along this coast of ours. I heard Dixon—on Death ;—somewhat in King Cambyses' vein.— He is a witcracker by profession—otherwise a good fellow enough. Between ourselves, our own minister here is the veriest drug that ever hapless audience yawned under. He has ingine¹ too—but as much laziness along with it as might suffice for a Presbytery. I protest if he become no better, I shall be compelled to abandon him, in a great measure. Yesterday all the world was in mourning—and hearing sermons for the Princess Charlotte. I was much struck with the fate of that exalted person. Her age was within a month of my own. A few days ago she was

> " As full of spirit as the month of May ;   —
> And gorgeous as the sun at Midsummer "—

and now ! Truly pale Death overturns, with impartial foot, the hut of the poor man and the palace of the King.

It is past midnight—so I shall have done. Greet Mrs. Church and Miss Harper in my name. Mr. Church will prefer an account of the harvest to compliments. Therefore let him know that the state of Agricultural affairs in this district is very pitiful : the crops are backward to a degree that is quite unaccountable—and not paralleled by any season within

---

¹ Scotch for " genius " or " mind " in general.

the memory of man.   Part of the oats is uncut ;
and the whole country hereabout and westward,
as I learn, is covered with shocks.   The weather
is moist too—so that altogether the Husbandman has an afflicting prospect. . . .

To-morrow I go to Edinburgh with Irving.
If we get safe over, you will find it noted in
the vacant space.   Meantime I'll to my truckle-
bed.   I have nothing more to tell you, but that
I am as heretofore, yours truly,

THOMAS CARLYLE.

XXI.—To Mr. R. MITCHELL, Ruthwell Manse.

KIRKCALDY, *16th February* 1818.

After an arduous struggle with sundry his-
torians of great and small renown, I sit down
to answer the much-valued epistle of my friend.
Doubtless you are disposed to grumble that I
have been so long in doing so ; but I have an
argument in store for you.   To state the proposition logically—this letter, I conceive, must
either amuse you or not.   If it amuse you—
then certainly you cannot be so unreasonable

as to cavil at a little harmless delay: and if it do not—you will rather rejoice that your punishment has not been sooner inflicted. Having thus briefly fixed you between the horns of my dilemma—from which, I flatter myself, no skill will suffice to extricate you—I proceed with a peaceful and fearless mind.

My way of life is still after the former fashion. I continue to teach (that I may subsist thereby), with about as much satisfaction as I should beat hemp, if such were my vocation. Excepting one or two individuals, I have little society that I value very highly, but books are a ready and effectual resource. May blessings be upon the head of Cadmus or the Phœnicians, or whoever invented books! I may not detain you with the praises of an art that carries the voice of man to the extremities of the earth, and to the latest generations, but it is lawful for the solitary wight to express the love he feels for those companions so stedfast and unpresuming—that go or come without reluctance, and that, when his fellow animals are proud or stupid or peevish, are ever ready to cheer the languor of his soul, and gild the barrenness of life with the treasures of bygone times. Now and then I cross the Frith : but these expeditions are not attended with much enjoyment. The time has been when I would have stood a-tiptoe at the name of Edinburgh,— but all that is altered now. The men with whom I meet are mostly preachers or students in divinity. These persons desire, not to understand Newton's philosophy, but to obtain a well 'plenished manse. Their ideas, which are uttered with much vain jangling, and generally couched in a recurring series of quips and most slender puns, are nearly confined to the church or rather kirk-session politics of the place, the secret habits, freaks, and adven- · tures of the clergy or professors, the vacant parishes and their presentees, with patrons, tutors, and all other appurtenances of the tythe-pig-tail. Such talk is very edifying certainly : but I take little delight in it. My Theological-propensities may be enclosed within very small compass—and with regard to witlings, jibers or such small deer—the less one knows of them,—

it is not the worse. Yet there are some honest persons with whom I spend sometimes an afternoon comfortably enough. Before leaving this subject I wish to ask how *your* theological studies are advancing—and chiefly when you are to be at Kirkcaldy? I doubt my career "in the above line" has come to a close. Perhaps I have already told you that there are a thousand preachers on the field at present. Now from calculations founded on *data* furnished me by persons well versed in these matters—and managed by the rules laid down in Dilworth—I find that the last draught of these expectants, supposing *no new* ones to appear in the interim, will at their settlement be upon the verge of their grand climacteric. After which, the "prospects of being useful" cannot, one would think, be very bright.

I am sorry that Mathematics cause *hepatitis* in you. The pursuit of truth is certainly the most pleasing and harmless object that can engage the mind of man in this troublous world : and where shall we find her in her native purity, if not in the science of quantity and number ? I counsel you to resume your operations as soon as your cranium will permit —which I trust will happen without loss of time. You will thank me, no doubt, for this sage advice ; but if you knew the need I have of it myself, you would be the more disposed to admire my generosity. It is long since I told you I had begun Wallace, and that foreign studies had cast him into the shade. The same causes still obstruct my progress. You will perhaps be surprised that I am even now no farther advanced than "the circle of curvature." I have found his demonstrations circuitous but generally rigorous. Yet I must except the proof of Maclaurin's theorem in page 414—which, if I were not a little man and Wallace a great, I should have small hesitation to pronounce unsatisfactory, not to say absurd. I suppose I had read Hume's *England* when I wrote last ; and I need not repeat my opinion of it. My perusal of the continuation—eight volumes, of history, as it is called, by Tobias Smollett, M.D., and others, was a much harder and more unprofitable task. Next I read

Gibbon's *Decline and Fall of the Roman Empire*—a work of immense research and splendid execution. Embracing almost all the civilised world, and extending from the time of Trajan to the taking of Constantinople by Mahomet II. in 1453, it connects the events of ancient with those of modern history. Alternately delighted and offended by the gorgeous colouring with which his fancy invests the rude and scanty materials of his narrative; sometimes fatigued by the learning of his notes, occasionally amused by their liveliness, frequently disgusted by their obscenity, and admiring or deploring the bitterness of his skilful irony—I toiled through his massy tomes with exemplary patience. His style is exuberant, sonorous, and epigrammatic to a degree that is often displeasing. He yields to Hume in elegance and distinctness—to Robertson in talents for general disquisition—but he excels them both in a species of brief and shrewd remark for which he seems to have taken Tacitus as a model, more than any other that I know of.[1] The

---

[1] "Irving's library was of great use to me," writes Carlyle,

whole historical triumvirate are abundantly
destitute of virtuous feeling—or indeed of any
feeling at all. I wonder what benefit is derived
from reading all this stuff. What business of
mine is it though Timur Beg erected a pyramid
of eighty thousand human skulls in the valley
of Bagdad, and made an iron cage for Bajazet.

"Gibbon, Hume, etc. etc. I think I must have read it almost
through ;—inconceivable to me now with what ardour, with
what greedy velocity, literally above ten times the speed I can
now make with any book. Gibbon, in particular, I recollect
to have read at the rate of a volume a day (twelve volumes in
all) ; and I have still a fair recollection of it, though seldom
looking into it since. It was of all the books, perhaps, the
most impressive on me in my then stage of investigation and
state of mind. I by no means completely admired Gibbon,
perhaps not more than I now do, but his winged sarcasms,
so quiet and yet so conclusively transpiercing and killing dead,
were often admirable, potent, and illuminative to me. Nor did
I fail to recognise his great power of investigating, ascertain-
ing, of grouping and narrating ; though the latter had always,
then as now, something of a Drury Lane character, the colours
strong but coarse, and set off by lights from the side scenes.
We had books from Edinburgh College Library, too. (I
remember Bailly's *Histoire de l'Astronomie*, ancient and also
modern, which considerably disappointed me.) On Irving's
shelves were the small Didot French classics in quantity.
With my appetite sharp, I must have read of French and
English (for I don't recollect much classicality, only something of mathematics in intermittent spasms) a great deal
during those years."—*Reminiscences*, i. 102.

And what have I to do with the savage cold-
blooded policy of Charles, and the desolating
progress of either Zinghis or Napoleon? It is
in vain to tell us that our knowledge of human-
nature is increased by the operation. *Useful*
knowledge of that sort is acquired not by
reading but experience. And with regard to
political advantages—the less one knows of
them, the greater will be his delight in the
principles of my Lords Castlereagh and Sid-
mouth, with their circulars, suspensions, holy
leagues, and salvation of Europe. Yet if not
profit there is some *pleasure* in history at all
events. I believe we must not apply the *cui-
bono* too rigorously. It may be enough to
sanction any pursuit, that it gratifies an innocent and still more an honourable propensity of
the human mind. When I look back upon
this paragraph, I cannot but admit that re-
viewing is a very beneficial art. If a dull man
take it into his head to write either for the
press or the post office, without materials—at a
dead lift, it never fails to extricate him. But
too much of one thing—as it is in the adage.

Therefore I reserve the account of Hume's
Essays till another opportunity. At any rate
the second volume is not finished yet—and I do
not like what I have read of it anything [like]
so well as I did the first. Neither would it be
profitable to tell you the faults of *Godwin's*
powerful but unnatural and bombastic novel [1]
—or to sing the praises of *Rob Roy*—which
you have no doubt read and admired sufficiently already. Nor will I say one word
about the swarms of magazines, pamphlets,
and observations, which like the snow that
falls in the river, are one moment white, then
lost for ever. Here ends my chapter of re-
viewing.

Though possessing a sufficient confidence
in the efficacy of my dilemma, I dare hardly
venture to *demand* a speedy answer to this
letter. But I do entreat you to overcome the
vis inertiæ which adheres to mind as well as
matter—and send me some account of yourself
with all the velocity imaginable. You will be

[1] Godwin's now hardly remembered novel, *Mandevelle*, was
published in 1817.

through Russell before now. I long to hear your estimate of his merits[1] before I try him. I am thankful for your remarks upon Hunt and Hazlitt. Except through the medium of newspapers and reviews, I have no acquaintance with them. Hazlitt is somewhat celebrated for his essay on "Fine Arts" in the supplement to the *Encyclopædia Britannica;* and for his critique on "Standard Novels" in the *Edinburgh Review.* I know not whether you have heard anything of Playfair's new demonstration (for such he protests it is) of the composition of forces—I have no room for it now. But if you like you shall have it next time—together with the wonderful *slide* upon mount Pilatus in the canton of Lucerne for conveying timber to the lake—which he examined whilst travelling in foreign parts—and described when I was in his class, with great complacency. Do you ever see that sluggish person Johnstone of Hitchill? I protest—but there is not space for protesting. Tell him simply to write instanter if he wish his head

[1] Russell's *History of Modern Europe.*

to continue above his *hass-bone*.[1]—I remain, my
dear Mitchell, yours faithfully,

THOMAS CARLYLE.

(Send a letter quickly, an thou love me.)

XXII.—To Mr. R. MITCHELL, Ruthwell Manse.

KIRKCALDY, 25*th May* 1818.

MY DEAR FRIEND—After parting with you
on the quay of Burntisland, I proceeded slowly
to the eastward; and seating myself upon the
brow of that crag from which the poor King
Alexander *brak's neck-bane*,[2] I watched your
fleet-sailing skiff till it vanished in the mists
of the Forth. So Mitchell is gone! thought I,
we shall have no more chat together for many

[1] Neck.
[2] "As he [Alexander III.] was riding in the dusk of the
evening along the sea-coast of Fife, betwixt Burntisland and
Kinghorn, he approached too near the brink of the precipice,
and his horse starting or stumbling, he was thrown over the
rock and killed on the spot. It is now no less than five
hundred and forty-two years since Alexander's death [in 1285],
yet the people of the country still point out the very spot where
it happened, and which is called the King's Crag."—*Tales of
a Grandfather*, ch. vi.

a day ; but he will write me a letter in a week
at any rate : and with that consolatory expectation, I pensively returned to Kirkcaldy.
If excessive studiousness has frustrated this
hope, then it is well, and I shall wait con-
tentedly till some hour of relaxation occur,
when you may sport upon paper for my
benefit—without detriment to your graver
pursuits.   But if sheer indolence possesses
you, it were proper to cast off the noxious
spell, as soon as possible.   From the fact of
my writing at present, you may conjecture (and
rightly) that my own avocations are slackly
pursued.   My conduct, I fear, is absurd.   I
believe it to be a truth (and though no creature
believed it, it would continue to be a truth)
that a man's dignity in the great system of
which he forms a part is exactly proportional
to his moral and intellectual acquirements : and
I find moreover, that when I am assaulted by
those feelings of discontent and ferocity which
solitude at all times tends to produce, and by
that host of miserable little passions which are
ever and anon attempting to disturb one's re-

pose, there is no method of defeating them so effectual as to take them in flank by a zealous course of study. I *believe* all this—but my practice clashes with my creed. I had read some little of Laplace when I saw you ; and I continue to advance with a diminishing velocity. I turned aside into Leslie's *Conics*—and went through it, in search of two propositions, which, when in your geometrical vein, you will find little difficulty in demonstrating. Take them if you will. [Propositions omitted.] . . .

I likewise also turned aside into Charles Bossut's *Mécanique*—to study his demonstration of pendulums, and his doctrine of forces. The text is often tediously explanatory—and in the notes it is but a dim hallucination of the truth that I can obtain through the medium of integrals and differentials by which he communicates it. However, I am now pretty well convinced that a body projected from the earth with a velocity of 39,000 feet per second will never return. I got Lagrange's *Mécanique Analytique* also, but to me it is nearly a sealed book. After all these divarications, and more

which I shall mention afterwards, you must
pardon me if I am not above half through the
Exposition du système du monde. The first
volume is beautiful, and can be understood;
great part of the second is demonstrated, he
says, in the *Mécanique celeste,* and I am obliged
to be content with ignorantly admiring these
sublime mysteries which I am assured are *de
hautes connaissances, les delices des êtres pensans.*
Surely it *is* a powerful instrument which en-
ables the mind of a man to grasp the universe
and to elicit from it and demonstrate such laws
—as that, whatever be the actions of the
planets on each other, the mean distances of
each from the sun and its mean motion can
never change : and that, *every* variation in *any*
of their elements must be periodical. To see
these truths, my good Robert—to *feel* them as
one does the proportions of the sphere and
cylinder! 'Tis a consummation devoutly to
be wished—but not very likely ever to arrive.
Sometimes, indeed, on a fine evening, and
when I have quenched my thirst with large
potations of Souchong, I say to myself—away

with despondency—hast thou not a soul and a
kind of understanding in it ? And what more
has any analyst of them all ? But next morning, alas, when I consider my understanding—
how coarse yet feeble it is, and how much of it
must be devoted to supply the vulgar wants of
life, or to master the paltry but never-ending
vexations with which all creatures are be-
leaguered—I ask how is it possible not to
despond ? Especially, when, as old Chaucer
said of the *Astrolaby*,[1] "the conclusions that
have been founden or ells possiblye might be
founde in so noble an instrument, ben un-
knowen perfitely to any mortal man in this
region, as I suppose." But I fear you are
tired of these prosings—you must bear with
them. Excepting the few friends whom Providence has given me, and whose kindness I
wish never to forfeit, I have and am likely to
have little else but these pursuits to derive
enjoyment from ; and there is none but you to

---

[1] *Vide* his treatise of the Astrolaby, "compowned for oure
orizont after the latitude of Oxenforde," to instruct "lytel
Lowis my sonne."—T. C.

talk it over with. They are all preaching here,—
and care not a straw for Laplace and his calculus both. You will be preaching one of these
days too—and perhaps—but it is needless to
anticipate—you must not leave off Mathematics.

Moore's *Lalla Rookh* and Byron's *Childe* ·
Harold (canto fourth) formed an odd mixture
with these speculations. It was foolish, you
may think, to exchange the truths of philosophy
for the airy nothings of these sweet singers :
but I could not help it. Do not fear that I
will spend time in criticising the *tulip cheek*.
Moore is but a sort of refined Mahometan, and
(with immense deference) I think that his character in a late *Edinburgh Review* [1] is somewhat too high. His imagination seldom quits
material, even sexual objects—he describes
them admirably,—and intermingles here and
there some beautiful traits of natural pathos ;
but he seems to have failed (excepting partially
in the Fire-Worshippers) in his attempts to
portray the fierce or lofty features of human

[1] In an article on *Lalla Rookh*, by Jeffrey, November 1817.

character. Mokannah in particular, insensible
to pain or pity or any earthly feeling, might
as well, at least for all practical purposes,
have been made of clockwork as of flesh and
blood. I grieve to say that the catastrophe
excited laughter rather than horror. The
poisoned believers sitting round the table,
with their black swollen jobber-nowls reclining
on their breasts, and saucer-eyes fixed upon
the ill-favoured prophet—appeared so like the
concluding scene of an election-dinner, when all
are dead-drunk but the Provost, a man of five
bottles, with a carbuncled face, and an amor-
phous nose, that I was forced to exclaim, *Du
sublime au ridicule il n'y a qu'un pas.* Moore
is universally said to be the author of *Letters
from the Fudge Family*—a work, if I may judge
by copious extracts, of extraordinary humour.
Phil Fudge seems to mean poor Southey. I
perceive, Mitchell, that I cannot finish this
letter in time for the post as I intended, and
since there is still a streak of radiance on the
horizon's brim, I may as well go forth to enjoy
it. Therefore good-bye, my old friend, for a

short season. 8½ o'clock P.M.—11 o'clock—I
return from a saunter with Pears, and an unprofitable inspection of his chaotic library, to
conclude my task. *Pennam* amens capio; nec -
sat rationis in *penna*. Be easy in your mind;
I am going to *write*, not *fly*. That dissertation
upon the Eastern Romance is so long-winded
that I cannot in conscience afflict you with
any remarks upon the deep-toned but [word
illegible] poetry of Lord Byron. What think
you of his address to Alphonso duke of Ferrara,
the persecutor of Tasso?

> " *Thou !* formed to eat, and be despised and die,
> Even as the beasts that perish, save that thou
> Hadst a more splendid trough and wider sty :
> *He !* etc."

This is emphatic enough. I need not speak
of Dr. Chalmers' boisterous treatise upon the-
causes and cure of pauperism in the last *Edinburgh Review*. His reasoning (so they call it)
is disjointed or absurd—and his language a
barbarous jargon—agreeable neither to Gods
nor men. And what avail the Church politics
of the General Assembly—the performances of

the fire-proof signora (Geraldini?)—or the fla-
gellations of Bill Blackwood, and the as paltry
antagonist of Bill Blackwood? But let me
repress these effusions of vanity;—pleasant
they may be to myself—yet unbecoming—till
I turn a renowned man—which unless things
be miserably conducted—will certainly (one
would think) come to pass one way or another.
What is the matter with Johnstone? He is
becoming very unguidable—and declines apparently either to *hop or win*—in the way of
writing letters. If you will not write to me
yourself, Mr. Robert, I cannot help it, but must
continue though " *without the least prefar-
ment,*" to subscribe myself your faithful but
disconsolate friend,

THOMAS CARLYLE.

XXIII.—To Mr. JAMES JOHNSTONE.

KIRKCALDY, 26*th June* 1818.

DEAR JOHNSTONE—It is about three weeks
since, after entering my chamber on a Sunday
evening, wearied with the toil, and sick with the

inanity of an excursion to Edinburgh, my eyes
were rejoiced with a sight of your letter. I
must not exchange the sentiments with which
you commence ; the partiality of friendship, and
the modesty of him who feels it, may become
excessive without ceasing to be amiable. I
have little genius for the complimentary, and,
therefore, shall not say in what esteem I hold
your communications,—let it be sufficient to
observe that the emotions they awaken are
among the happiest of my life, and that you
write so seldom is the very subject of complaint.

My journey to Edinburgh, you have learned,
was productive of little enjoyment. How should
it indeed ? Most of my acquaintances are looking out for kirks ; some by diligent pedagogy,
accompanied by a firm belief in the excellence
of certain country gentlemen, and others by
assiduously dancing attendance upon the leading clergymen of our venerable Establishment.
This is as it should be ; but I have no part or
lot in the matter. The rest speak of the St.
Ann - street - buildings, the *Brownie of Bodsbeck*, with other tales by James Hogg, and

things of that stamp. Now, the St. Ann-street-
buildings concern only some feuars of the ex-
tended royalty; and as for the *Brownie of*
Bodsbeck, with other tales by James Hogg,
they seem to have been written under the influence of a liquor more potent than that of the .
Pierian spring. So there needs not be much
said about them. If I go to the bookseller's
shop I find polemical Sciolists and pathetic
beaux-esprits. And when I walk along the
streets I see fair women, whom it were a folly
to think of for a moment, and fops (dandies as
they are called in current slang), shaped like an
hour-glass—creatures whose life and death, as
Crispin pithily observes, "I esteem of like importance, and decline to speak of either." It
would be ridiculous to fret at this. Being a
person of habits—I fear somewhat anomalous—
belonging to no profession, and waiting, therefore, on no idol of the tribe, or rather fashion-
able one, to bow down before, it is but little
sympathy I can look for.

I am far from laughing at your agricultural
studies, nor is it wonderful that you dislike

teaching—a lover of it is rare. No trade—but why do I talk? Discontent is the most vulgar of all feelings. It is utterly useless, moreover, more than useless. Let us cultivate our minds, and await the issue calmly, whatever it may be. The honest Hibernian had nothing to support himself, his wife, and children, nothing but these four bones. Yet he did not mourn nor despair.

Your project of a tour to the Cumberland Lakes meets my mind exactly. Get matters arranged, and I shall gladly accompany you to Keswick or Ulleswater, or wheresoever you please. . . . You must endeavour to have the route marked out before this night five weeks. On Saturday, the 1st of August, if all goes well, I hope to see you at Mainhill. You must be there any way if it be in your power.

The last book worth mentioning which I have perused was Stewart's *Preliminary Dissertation*, for the second time. The longer I study the works of this philosopher, the more I become convinced of two things—first, that in perspicacity and comprehension of understanding he yields to several; but, secondly, that in

taste, variety of acquirements, and what is of
more importance, in moral dignity of mind,
he has no rival that I know of. Every liberal
opinion has at all times found in him a zealous
advocate. When he has come before the public
he has borne himself with a carriage so meek,
yet so commanding, and now, when, with unabating ardour, he is retired to devote the last
remnant of his well-spent life to the great cause
of human improvement, his attitude is so pensively sublime, I regard him with a reverence
which I scarcely feel for any other living person.
He is a man, take him for all in all, we shall
not look upon his like again. There is something melancholy in the thought that the world
cannot long enjoy the light of such a mind.
But the cup goes round, and who so artful as
to put it by. Poor Donaldson, you see, is cut
off in the prime of his days. Poor fellow, few
summers have passed since he was my companion, as careless, good-natured a being as
ever breathed the air of this world. And to
think that he is gone excites many painful reflections upon the obvious but solemn truth

that the place which now knows us will ere
long know us no more at all, for ever. It is
foolish, we are told, to shrink from, or repine at
the unalterable fate to which this earth and those
that it inherit have been doomed. It is un-
speakably ungrateful, too, for who would wish
to live thus for ever? And one year or a
thousand centuries are the same fleeting instant
in the everlasting sweep of ages that have been
and are to come.

"Ex Asia rediens (says Servius Sulpicius in his far-famed
letter to Tully) cum ab Aegina Megaram versus navigarem,
cœpi regiones circumcirca prospicere. Post nos erat Aegina,
ante Megara, dextrâ Piræeus, sinistrâ Corinthus; quæ
oppida quodam tempore florentissima fuerunt, nunc pros-
trata ac diruta ante oculos jacent. Cœpi egomet mecum sic
cogitare: Hem! nos homunculi indignamur, si quis nostrûm
interiit aut occisus est quorum vita brevior esse debet, cum
uno loco tot oppidorum cadavera projecta jacent! Visne
tu te, Servi, cohibere, et meminisse, hominem te esse
natum?"

All this may be true philosophy, yet still
some internal tears will fall on the graves of
those whom we have loved, and who are
departed to that land of darkness, and of the
shadow of death, about which so much is hoped

or feared and so little understood. Those are
mournful thoughts. They come across my
mind at times in the stillness of the solitary
night, and plunge me into an ocean of fearful
conjectures. "My God," exclaims the melancholy and high-minded Pascal, "enlighten my
soul or take from it this reasoning curiosity."
Montaigne tells us that he "reposed upon the
pillow of doubt." And there is a day coming—
it is even now not far distant—when all mine
shall be explained or need no explanation. I
will pursue these reflections no further. One
thing, let us never cease to believe whatever be
our destiny—an upright mind is the greatest
blessing we can obtain or imagine.—Believe me
to be, yours faithfully,   THOMAS CARLYLE.

XXIV.—To Mr. THOMAS MURRAY, Manse of
    Sorbie, by Wigtown, Galloway.

KIRKCALDY, 28*th July* 1818.

MY DEAR SIR — Whilst arranging some
scattered papers previously to my departure
from this place, which I am to leave to-morrow

for Dumfriesshire, I happened to alight upon
your letter. The recollection that it was un-
answered awakened a feeling of remorse in my
mind; and though it is near midnight, I have
determined to employ the passing hour by
writing you a few lines by way of a return
for your affectionate farewell. If I have
not done so sooner, impute it, I beseech you,
to want of ability rather than of inclination.
Be assured, I have not forgotten the many joy-
ful days which long ago we spent together—
sweet days of ignorance and airy hope! They
had their troubles too: but to bear them, there
was a light-heartedness and buoyancy of soul,
which the sterner qualities of manhood, and the
harsher buffetings that require them, have for
ever forbidden to return.

I forbear to say much of the pursuits which
have engaged me. They would little interest
you, I fear. With most young men, I have had
dreams of intellectual greatness, and of making
me a name upon the earth. They were little
else but dreams. To gain renown is what I
do not hope, and hardly care for, in the present

state of my feelings. The improvement of
one's mind, indeed, is the noblest object which
can occupy any reasonable creature : but the
attainment of it requires a concurrence of circumstances over which one has little control.
I now perceive more clearly than ever, that any
man's opinions depend not on himself so much
as on the age he lives in, or even the
persons with whom he associates. If his mind
at all surpass their habits, his aspirings are
quickly quenched in the narcotic atmosphere
that surrounds him. He forfeits sympathy, and
procures hatred if he excel but a little the dull
standard of his neighbours. Difficulties multi-
ply as he proceeds ; and none but chosen souls
can rise to any height above the level of the
swinish herd. Upon this principle, I could tell
you why Socrates sacrificed at his death to
Esculapius—why Kepler wrote his *Cosmo-
graphic Harmony*, and why Sir Thomas More
believed the Pope to be infallible. Nevertheless one should do what he can.

I need not trouble you with the particulars
of my situation. My prospects are not ex-

tremely brilliant at present. I have quitted all
thoughts of the church, for many reasons, which
it would be tedious, perhaps displeasing, to
enumerate. I feel no love (I should wish to
see the human creature that feels any love) for
the paltry trade I follow; and there is before
me a chequered and fluctuating scene, where I
see nothing clearly, but that a little time will
finish it. Yet wherefore should we murmur?
A share of evil greater or less (the difference of
shares is not worth mentioning) is the unalterable doom of mortals: and the mind may be
taught to abide it in peace. Complaint is
generally despicable, always worse than unavailing. It is an instructive thing, I think, to
observe Lord Byron surrounded with the
voluptuousness of an Italian Seraglio, chaunting
a mournful strain over the wretchedness of
human life; and then to contemplate the poor
but lofty-minded Epictetus—the slave—of a
cruel master too—and to hear him lifting up
his voice to far distant generations, in these
unforgotten words: Ἀπαιδεύτου ἔργον, τὸ ἄλλοις
ἐγκαλεῖν, ἐφ᾽ οἷς αὐτὸς πράσσει κακῶς · ἠργμένου

παιδεύεσθαι, τὸ ἑαυτῷ · πεπαιδευμένου, τὸ μήτ' ἄλλῳ, μήθ' ἑαυτῷ.[1] But truce to moralising—suffice it, with our Stoic to say, ἀνέχου καὶ ἀπέχου, which, being interpreted, is *suffer and abstain.*

I heard with pleasure that you had got *licence*, and had preached with success. May you soon obtain a settlement, and feel happy in it. A Scottish clergyman, when he does his duty faithfully, is both a useful and honourable member of society. When he neglects his office, and has subscribed his creed "with a sigh or a smile" (as Gibbon spitefully remarks) —the less one says of him the better. But I hope other things of you.

Three weeks ago I had a visit from the forlorn Poet Stewart Lewis. He came into the school one morning, and stood plumb up without speaking a word. I was touched to see the gray veteran, in tattered clothes, and with a pensive air, waging against necessity the same unprosperous battle which, any time these forty

[1] "It is the way of an uninstructed man to blame others for what falls out ill for him ; of one beginning to be instructed to blame himself, but of one well-instructed to blame neither another nor himself."—*Encheiridion*, c. v.

years, has been his constant occupation. His
wife died many months ago; and since that
event he has been protracting a miserable, useless existence (he called it) by selling small
poems of his own composing. I understand he
got rid of some part of his cargo here;—and of
all his sorrows, by a copious potation of *usquebaugh.* He spoke to me with much gratitude
of a certain young lady in Wigton, who for
your sake (I think of that Master Brook) had
sought out his lodgings and replenished his
purse. He has many faults, and the crowning
one of drunkenness—but some genius likewise,
and a degree of taste, which, considering his
habits and situation, is altogether surprising.
Moreover he is old, and poor, and not unthankful for any kindness shown him. I pity the
man and would not wish to see him die a
mendicant.[1]

[1] Mitchell writing to Carlyle, on the 12th of October, says,
"You would probably see by the Newspapers the death of
poor Stewart Lewis. He had been somewhere about Max-
welltown tasting a little of his dear *usquebaugh.* He fancied
his face dirty (I have this account from his son), and, with
laudable desire to get it cleaned, went to the Nithside, where,
stooping too low, he toppled headlong, and with difficulty re-

Perhaps you are acquainted with the tragic
end of poor William Irving whom you once
knew. Though auguring little good of him, I
never feared that he would do that deed, which
renders his name a thing which sober people
may not mention. But now that it has happened, suicide seems a not unsuitable conclusion
to his frantic and miserable way of life. I
bewail his mournful destiny. Had the talents
which he certainly did possess been cultivated
with judgment, and directed by principle of
any kind—he might have been a credit to his
country.

If you write to me before September, let
your letter be directed to Mainhill near Ecclefechan—after that period, to Mrs. Skeens,
Kirkwynd, Kirkcaldy. Are you to leave Sorbie?

gained the side. Though his clothes were hung before a fire
during the night, they were still wet next day ; an inflam-
matory fever ensued, and Lewis ended his changeful life
in a low lodging-house in the village of Ruthwell. The least
thing that I could do was to attend the funeral of him who
had dedicated his poems to the Students of his native Annandale. He was decently interred in this churchyard, where
a stone with a suitable inscription, as is customary in cases
of this kind, is about to be erected to his memory."

I must hear of your destination. During the vacation I intend to visit the Cumberland Lakes; and I should like to see Galloway also, but I cannot make it out this Summer. Will you be in Edinburgh any time soon? When or where shall I see you? Write me a letter at least when you can find leisure, and believe me to be, my dear Murray, yours faithfully,

THOMAS CARLYLE.

XXV.—To his FATHER.

KIRKCALDY, *2d September* 1818.

MY DEAR FATHER—Having arrived in safety at this place, I sit down to give you an account of my adventures by the way—and my proceedings since I left the Mainhill. After shaking hands with Sandy I winded down the Baileyhill, easily forded the Black Esk, and proceeded along the banks of its sister stream to Eskdalemoor-manse, which I reached about seven o'clock. I cast many an anxious thought after Sandy and the horses which he was conducting: but I hope they arrived in safety

after all. The minister is a kind, hospit-
able man. Saturday morning was wet, and he
would fain have persuaded me to stay all day
with him, but when he could not succeed he
spread before me a large map of Dumfriesshire,
pointed out the best road, and gave me a line
to one Anderson (a cousin of his wife), from
whom I was to get some meat as I passed
Lyart upon Meggat water. After my departure the rain slackened a little, but the hilltops
were covered with a dark mist which the wind
tossed about briskly. I proceeded up the Esk,
which originates about six miles above the
manse in the junction of two streams, the Tom-
leuchar and the Glenderg—of which the latter
rises near the eastern edge of Ettrick Pen, the
former a few miles eastward. Ascending Glenderg I came into Ettrick water, which I crossed
at a place called Cosser's hill, where a hospit-
able but sluttish and inquisitive old woman
gave me some potatoes, etc., with directions
for finding Kiskenhope—the head of the two
Lochs (St. Mary's and the Lowes) upon Yarrow
water, distant about four miles. I was upon

the brow of a solitary ridge of moorland hills when I saw the two clear blue lakes, and in about half an hour I had crossed the stream which unites them, and was upon the road up Meggat, a brook which rises a little to the north of Whitecomb, and joins the eastermost lake (St. Mary's) after a course of about six miles. When I got to Anderson's at Lyart it was almost seven o'clock, and his sister pressed me much to stay all night, the man (an arrant miser as I found afterwards) did not press me so keenly. As it was raining a little, and Peebles fourteen miles distant, I thought of accepting their invitation, and having got some tea was endeavouring to enter into some conversation with this rich old farmer. But when he perceived that I was going to continue with him all night he became so churlish in his replies that I could think of it no longer, and taking my hat and stick I thanked him for his entertainment, and crossed the water of Meggat, leaving this Nabal of Yarrow with his sister in utter amazement at my departure, for it was now near eight, and the night was rainy. But

in half an hour I came into road which I had
travelled over before (as I came down), and
though the rain continued, I reached the house
of a kind herdsman upon Manor water (which
comes into the Tweed near Peebles), and met
with a warm reception from him, after nine
o'clock. Next morning was dry, and the day
became windy : so I arrived at Edinburgh that
same afternoon about five—and staid all night
with Donaldson—formerly Irving's assistant at
Kirkcaldy. Next day I saw Mr. Leslie, who—
was very kind, and got me a book that I was
wanting from the library, and talked with me
about two hours very frankly. I also purchased
for my kind Mother a black bonnet with ribands
and other equipments, which the people engaged
to put into a box and send by Gavin Johnston
the Annan carrier. I hope she will accept of
it for my sake, who owe her so much. It is
directed to the care of Robert Brand, Lockerbie.
I enclose you a draught for £15, which you
will know how to dispose of. It is not likely
that I shall feel any want of it at present, and
no one can have a better right to it than you.

My prospects in this place are far from
brilliant at present. About a month before I
went away, a body had established himself in
my neighbourhood, and taken up a school, but
could make next to nothing of it. During the
vacation, however, he seems to have succeeded
in getting most of my scholars—and to-day I
mustered only twelve. This will never do.
The people's rage for novelty is the cause of it,
I suppose, for the poor creature is very ignorant,
and very much given to drink. I make no
doubt I could re-establish the school, but the
fact is I am very much tired of the trade, and
very anxious to find some other way of making
my bread, and this is as good a time for trying
it as any other. Irving is going away too, and
I shall have no associate in the place at all. I
think I could find private teaching perhaps
about Edinburgh to support me till I could fall
into some other way of doing. At any rate, I
have more than seventy pounds (besides what
I send you) of ready money, and that might
keep me for a season. In short, I only wait for
your advice, till I give in my resignation against

the beginning of December. I have thought of trying the law, and several other things, but I have not yet got correct information about any of them. Give my kindest love to all my brothers and sisters. I expect a letter very soon, for I shall be unhappy till I resolve upon something. In the meantime, however, I remain, my dear Father, yours affectionately,

· THOMAS CARLYLE.

I have not yet seen much of the country, but the crops seem more backward than in Dumfriesshire. They are busy exporting potatoes from this place to England—what part I know not—so the article will probably be dear.

XXVI.—From his MOTHER.

MAINHILL, 31*st October* 1818.

DEAR TOM—You will by this time be thinking that I have forgot you quite, but far from that you are little out of my mind. I have sent your socks; they are not so fine as I could have wished, not having as much [wool] as could be done on the mill, but I hope they will do for the winter. I received the bonnet; it is a very good one. I doubt it would be very high. I can only thank you at this time. I have been rather uneasy about your settlement, but seek direction alway from Him who can give it aright, and may He be thy guide, Tom. I have been very uneasy about your things being so long in going off, but one disappointment after another it is so. Tell me if anything else is wanting that is in my power and I will get it you. I have reason to be thankful I am still in good health and spirits, yet I would be gratified much to hear of you comfortably settled nevertheless. Let us learn to submit, and take it as God is pleased to send it. It is a world of trouble at the best. Write me soon, Tom, do, and tell me all your news, good and bad. We have got all our crop in; it looks very well. I daresay you will have heard of Mrs. Calvert's death. She died soon after you went away, rather hastily. But I daresay I have as much written as you will be able to read well. Send me a long letter. Tell me honestly if thou reads a Chapter every day, and may the Lord bless and keep thee. I add no more, but remain your loving mother and sincere friend,

MARGARET CARLYLE.

XXVII.—To Mr. R. MITCHELL, Ruthwell Manse.

KIRKCALDY, *6th November* 1818.

MY DEAR MITCHELL—About a week ago I received a letter from the Magistrates of this burgh (which letter I even now use as a blot sheet) accepting my "resignation of the Teacher of the Grammar school," as their phrase goes : and in a fortnight, I shall quit my present situation. Although I relate this event so abruptly, my part in it has not been performed without profound deliberation. You shall hear it all. The miseries of school teaching were known long before the second Dionysius, who opened shop, in the city of Corinth, about the middle of the fourth century before Christ. Lucian— (the Voltaire of antiquity) has left his opinion, in writing, that when the Gods have determined to render a man ridiculously miserable, they make a schoolmaster of him ; and an experience of more than four years does not, in my own case, authorise me to contradict this assertion. But of late, the loss of my companions (Irving, who left us last Saturday, and Pears, who will depart in ten days), together with some convincing proofs of unpopularity, have given to my reflections on this subject a complexion more serious than ordinary.[1]   I have thought

[1] " In the space of two years," writes Carlyle in his *Reminiscences* (i. 140), " or rather more, we had all got tired of schoolmastering and its mean contradictions and poor results : Irving and I quite resolute to give it up for good ; the headlong Piers [*sic*] disinclined for it on the then terms longer, and in the end of 1819 (or '18 ? at this hour I know not which, and the old *Letters* which would show are too deep hidden), we all three went away ; Irving and I to Edinburgh, Piers to his own ' East Country '—whom I never saw again with eyes, poor good rattling soul.   Irving's outlooks in Edinburgh were not of the best, considerably checkered with dubiety, opposition, or even flat disfavour in some quarters ; but at least they were far superior to mine, and indeed, I was beginning my four or five most miserable, dark, sick, and heavy-laden years ; Irving, after some staggerings aback, his seven or eight healthiest and brightest.   He had, I should guess, as one item several good hundreds of money to wait upon.   My *peculium* I don't recollect, but it could not have exceeded £100.   I was without friends, experience, or connection in the sphere of human business, was of shy humour, proud enough and to spare, and had begun my long curriculum of dyspepsia, which has never ended since ! "

much and long of the irksome drudgery—the solitude—the gloom of my condition. I reasoned thus : These things may be endured, if not with a peaceful heart, at least with a serene countenance ; but it is worth while to inquire whether the profit will repay the pain of enduring them. A scanty and precarious livelihood constitutes the profit ; you know me, and can form some judgment of the pain. But there is loss as well as pain. I speak not of the loss of health : but the destruction of benevolent feeling, that searing of the heart, which misery, especially of a petty kind, sooner or later, will never fail to effect—is a more frightful thing. The desire, which, in common with all men, I feel for conversation and social intercourse, is, I find, enveloped in a dense repulsive atmosphere —not of vulgar *mauvaise honte*, though such it is generally esteemed—but of deeper feelings, which I partly inherit from nature, and which are mostly due to the undefined station I have hitherto occupied in society. If I continue a schoolmaster, I fear there is little reason to doubt that these feelings will increase, and at

last drive me entirely from the kindly sympa-—
thies of life, to brood in silence over the bitterness into which my friendly propensities must
be changed. Where *then* would be my comfort? Had I lived at Athens, in the plastic—
days of that brilliant commonwealth, I might
have purchased "a narrow paltry tub," and—
pleased myself with uttering gall among them
of Cynosarges.[1] But in these times—when—
political institutions and increased civilisation
have fixed the texture of society—when Religion has the privilege of prescribing principles
of conduct, from which it is a crime to dissent—
when, therefore, the aberrations of philosophical enthusiasm are regarded not with admiration
but contempt—when Plato would be dissected—
in the *Edinburgh Review*, and Diogenes laid
hold of by "a Society for the Suppression of
Beggars"—in these times—it may not be. But
this cure, or any other that I know of, not being
applicable, it were better to avoid the disease.
Therefore I must cease to be a pedagogue. The

---

[1] The gymnasium outside Athens where Antisthenes taught,
whence the Cynics, some say, derived their name.

question is now reduced within a narrower compass. It remains only to inquire at what time I can quit this employment, with the greatest chance of finding another. But how, except by some brisk sally, am I likely ever to emerge from my thraldom? Scantily supplied with books, without a rival or a comrade in the pursuit of anything scientific, little can be achieved in that direction. With none here even to *show* me the various ways of living in the world, much less to help me into any of them—reduced to contemplate the busy scene of life, through the narrow aperture of printed books, Damoetas being judge, I have a right— metaphorically speaking, to be his great Apollo ; inasmuch as I have found and occupied that station where the space of heaven extends not more than three ells.[1] The brightest of my days too are flying fast over my head ; and the sooner I resolve, the better. Besides at this time (that of Irving's departure) I give my em-

---

[1] " Dic, quibus in terris,—et eris mihi magnus Apollo—
Tris pateat coeli spatium non amplius ulnas."
                              Virgil, *Ecloga* iii. 104, 105.

ployers the fittest opportunity to erect an institution for education, that may end their woes
on that head—which, for the last six years, have
been neither few nor small.   In short the present is the time.   And I wrote my demission
on the 23d October accordingly.   After receiving the answer above alluded to, the business
seemed to be done; when on Monday last, a
certain very kind and worthy banker, Mr. Swan,
attended by another person, came to ask me,
whether if they could offer me a salary between
£120 and £150, for teaching, in a private
capacity, some thirty scholars, I would not be
induced to remain another year among them.
Upon my signifying an assent, they left me : to
procure subscribers, I suppose ; and I have
heard no more of their proceedings.   But for
this proposal, the probable success of which I
cannot estimate, and do not rate highly—
Edinburgh is certainly my destination for-the
winter.

I have calculated that, with economy, I
can live there for two years ; independently of
private teaching, which however I should not

refuse, if, as is not likely, it should offer itself.
During that period, if I do not study, I deserve
to continue ignorant. Mineralogy is to be my
winter's work. I have thought of writing for
booksellers. *Risum teneas;* for *at times* I am
serious in this matter. In fine weather it does
strike me that there are in this head some
ideas, a few *disjecta membra*, which might find
admittance into some one of the many publica-
tions of the day. To live by Authorship was
never my intention. It is said not to be
common at present ; and happily so : for if we
may credit biographers, the least miserable day
of an author's life is generally the last.

> ". . . Sad cure ! for who would lose,
> Though full of pain, this intellectual being,
> Those thoughts that wander through eternity,
> To perish rather, swallow'd up and lost
> In the wide womb of uncreated night,
> Devoid of sense and motion?"

I have meditated an attempt upon the profession of a lawyer, or of a civil engineer ; though
what person would afford me any assistance in
executing either of these projects, I cannot say.
It is doubtful if I can even learn the nature of the

obstacles to be overcome, and the recompense of success. This is the most provoking thing of all : yet how to remedy it ? I have thought of asking Mr. Duncan for an introduction to some of his friends in Edinburgh, who might *inform* me at least upon these points, help me to get books, and show me countenance in other ways that might not interfere with their own convenience. Tell me what you think of this. But do not mention it to Mr. D. ; he might regard it as an opening of the first parallel and *that* would be a mistake. When (if ever) I shall have convinced myself that it is right to overcome the scruples which one naturally feels against asking such a favour, for the first time in one's life I shall wish to execute the task, without any unnecessary meanness. The minister here is a worthy, kind man : but he has been beset with similar applications ; and I cannot trouble him. Last time I was in Edinburgh, I called at Professor Christison's, with full purpose of talking with him upon this subject : but the good man was already environed with a crowd of hungry schoolmasters. I felt

for myself—and made my exit in half an hour ;
though not till he had expounded the views of
Messieurs Dufief and Sabatier, and discussed
the merits of Sir James Mackintosh, the King,
the late Lord Hopetoun, Dr. Parr, the Calton-
hill observatory, with twenty other things, in
a way, which (no offence to the General) I
could not think very edifying.   Mr. Leslie has
already befriended me ; I must allow him to
"pursue the labyrinths of Physical research,"
without molestation.   Yet without some such
interference, I must be contented with *angels'*
visits to the College library, and my society
must consist of private teachers and proba-
tioners—a class of creatures (I speak it with
a sigh) not the least despicable in Edinburgh.   Their ideas are silly and grovelling,
their minds unvisited by any generous sentiments ; I love them not ; and of course, the
feeling will be mutual.

You see, my boy, that my prospects are not
the brightest in nature.   Yet what shall we
say ?   Contentment, that little practised virtue,—
has been inculcated by saint, by savage, and by

sage—and by each from a different principle.
Do not fear that I shall read you a homily on
that hackneyed theme.   Simply I wish to tell
you, that in days of darkness—for there *are*
days when my support (pride or whatever it is)
has enough to do—I find it useful to remember
that Cleanthes, whose ὕμνος εἰς τόν Θέον may
last yet another two thousand years, never
murmured, when he laboured by night as a
street porter, that he might hear the lectures of
Zeno by day; and that Epictetus, the ill-used
slave of a cruel tyrant's as wretched minion,
wrote that Enchiridion which may fortify the
soul of the latest inhabitant of Earth.   Besides,
though neither of these men had adorned their
species, it is morally certain that our earthly
joys or griefs can last but for a few brief years ;
and, though the latter were eternal, complaint
and despondency could neither mitigate their
intensity nor shorten their duration.   Therefore my duty, and that of every man, on this
point, is clear as light itself.

Excuse, my dear Mitchell, the egotism of
this almost interminable letter.   I have few

other friends before whom I can unfold my
secret soul. Do not say, with the French wit,
*on aime mieux dire du mal de soi-même, que de
n'en point parler.* Regard this rather as an
auricular confession, intended to answer, with
other purposes, that of marshalling my own
reasons for my conduct—that I may be the
better able to meet the result, whatever it be,
with a resolute spirit. · I have left myself no
room for criticism (falsely so called), or remarks
upon your interesting letter. How fully I par-
ticipate in your feelings with regard to the men
of Cambridge will appear from the foregoing
pages. Yet never despair. Remember Jere-
miah Horrox, John Kepler, Samuel Johnson,
and a cloud of other witnesses. Have you advanced far in Gibbon ? You would not, or will
not, fail to admire the characters of Stilicho, of
Aetius, of Boniface, of Belisarius—whilst the
threefold coffin of Attila the Hun, with the
barbaric splendour of his life and funeral, no
less than the boisterous spirit of Alaric the
Goth, whose bones *yet* repose beneath the
waves of the Cosenza, might inflame your

fancy with martial pomp and circumstance. What think you of Gibbon's views of the habits and opinions of those ages—his understanding —his style? I will not speak of Watson's history of the two Philips—an interesting, clear, well-arranged and rather feeble-minded work; any more than of the *Harrington and Ormond* of Edgeworth, or the chaotic jumble of Analytical institutions, Poems, Encyclopædias, Reviews, which of late I have grappled withal. I am glad to find you pleased with your Newton —the carriage was 1s. 8d., the residue I keep for you. Of course you will write to me before I leave this place—I say of course. I was going to ask whether our friend Johnstone was in the body—when lo! a letter from him reached me;—it shall be answered, tell him, in due time. I mourn for poor Lewis. Where is his son? Sir Samuel Romilly too! His peer is not within the empire. But I have done. Write (*obsecro*) in less than a week, to, my dear Mitchell, your faithful friend,

THOMAS CARLYLE.

XXVIII.—To Mr. R. MITCHELL, Ruthwell Manse.

EDINBURGH, 27*th November* 1818.

MY DEAR MITCHELL—Those who have never
known what it is to buffet with Fortune, and to
hear the voice of a friend encouraging them in
the strife, cannot understand the pleasure which
I felt from reading your letter.   It found me
on the eve of my departure from Kirkcaldy.
The plan of a subscription-school was, according to my expectation, given up for want of
subscribers.   I was packing my clothes and
books, writing directions, settling accounts,—
weighing anchor, in short, to venture once
again with little ballast, provision or experience,
upon the stormy ocean of life ; when your ad-
monitions came to shed a gleam of light athwart
my rough and doubtful course.   I thank you
for them, with all my soul.   If I have not done
it sooner, or if I do it now in a clumsy way—I
desire you to consider the trouble and vexation
which a change of place and habits produces :
and if this excuse will not satisfy you, add to it,
that for some days I have enjoyed very poor

health, which two ounces of sulphate of mag-
nesia which I swallowed two hours ago, have
not *yet* tended to diminish.

It would be ridiculous to affect displeasure
at your kind violation of my prohibition. You
have acted towards me as became a friend.
To Mr. Duncan, who possesses the rare talent
of conferring obligations without wounding the
vanity of him who receives them,—and the
still rarer disposition to exercise that talent—
all gratitude is due on my part. It is needless
to say more about my feelings upon this head.
With regard to the abilities which you are
kind enough to suppose that I possess for writing in Reviews and Encyclopædias—I have
much doubt : I have very little respecting the
alacrity with which I should engage in these
enterprises. At all events, I am highly indebted for all that has already been done in
that matter ; and shall receive with great
thankfulness the introductory letters which
you mention. The countenance and conversation of such a man as Dr. Brewster[1]

[1] Sir David Brewster.

cannot fail to be both gratifying and instructive to one in my circumstances. If I mistake
not, I have seen Mr. Henderson at Ruthwell
Manse. His manners seemed to be such as
become a gentleman. The information which
might be derived from him, concerning the
profession of law, is what I earnestly desire.

Perhaps you are curious to know the state
of my feelings at this crisis of my affairs. I
need not use many words to describe them.
Conceive to yourself a person of my stamp
(about which you should know something before this time) loosened from all his engagements with mankind, seated in a small room
in S. Richmond Street, revolving in his
altered soul the various turns of fate below—
whilst every time that the remembrance of his
forlorn condition comes across his brain, he
silently exclaims, "Why then the world's mine—
oyster; which I (not with *sword*, as Ancient
Pistol) will open"—as best I may: and you will
have some idea of my situation. I am not
unhappy:—for why? I have got Saussure's—
Voyages dans les Alpes; and it is my intention

to accompany him, before much time shall elapse, to the summit of the *Dôle* as well as to the *Col du Géant*. Besides, I have Irving to talk with about chemistry or the moral. sublime—Frances Dixon also, and Waugh, to spout poetry, not by weight and measure,—but in a plenteous way. There are others too—a numerous and nameless throng. I saw that admirable creature, Mr. Esbie, some weeks ago at Kirkcaldy. He came in company with one Galloway, a small dogmatical teacher of Mathematics—a wrangler of the first order— of brutal manners, and a terror to those embryo philosophers which (or rather who) frequent the backshop of David Brown. The contrast between this hirsute person and the double-refined travelling tutor was what Mr. E. him-self would have called *magnifique*. I thought of the little lap-dog, the dog of knowledge, which I had seen dancing in a ring with the rugged Russian bear. Esbie seems to have some good nature, and as his vanity, which is very considerable, lies quite in a different direction from one's own vanity (which in most cases is also considerable), he is, I should think, rather amusing than otherwise. To-day I saw him enter the College-yard—"and surely there never lighted upon this earth, which he scarcely seemed to touch, a more beauteous vision." I then thought (to continue in the words of Burke) that "ten thousand swords (fists rather) would have leapt from their scabbards to avenge even a look that threatened him with insult." But alas! poor Esbie must be content, he thinks, "*with some devil of a curacy*" as he calls it; though his acquaintance with "the first houses in Englànd" is of the most intimate nature.

I have heard Professor Jameson deliver two lectures. I am doubtful whether I ought to attend his class after all. He is one of those persons whose understanding is over-burthened by their memory. Destitute of accurate science, without comprehension of mind,—he details a chaos of facts, which he accounts for in a manner as slovenly as he selects and arranges them. Yesterday he explained the colour of the atmosphere,—upon principles which argued

a total ignorance of dioptrics. A knowledge of
the external character of minerals is all I can
hope to obtain from him.[1]

You will readily believe that I have not
read much since I wrote to you. Roscoe's
Life of Lorenzo de' Medici—a work concerning
which I shall only observe, in the words of the
Auctioneer, that it is "well worth any gentleman's perusal"—is the only thing almost that I
recollect aught about. I was grieved to read
your brief notice of your ill-health. I do hope
it is re-established. What says Newton? and
Gibbon? Have you given up *all* thoughts of
the Divinity Hall? Though there are few
persons on earth I desire as much to see, I
do not advise you to prosecute it. From the

---

[1] Professor Jameson's reputation was very high at this time
in Edinburgh. One may learn what was thought of him
from Lockhart's account in *Peter's Letters to his Kinsfolk* (i.
250), which were published in 1819. These Letters give
an entertaining picture of the Edinburgh of these years, well
worth comparing with Carlyle's incidental sketches. Chalmers,
Jeffrey, Playfair, Spurzheim, Leslie, Brewster,—all the Edinburgh notabilities—appear in the lively and flippant pages of
the brilliant and successful man of the world in different lights
and colours from those in which they were seen by the serious,
lonely, struggling student.

conversation which we had in the inn at Bassenthwaite Halls, and elsewhere, I judge that you are as unfit as myself for the study of Theology, as they arrogantly name it. Whatever becomes of us, let us never cease to behave like honest men.

When did you see Johnstone? I hope you often meet to point out, when other topics fail, the contour of that Alpine range in whose un-forgotten bosom we spent some days in so happy a manner. Certainly he will soon hear from me. I intended to have written him long ago.

I must have a letter from you as soon as your good nature will afford me that pleasure. Excuse the dulness of this epistle and its brevity (a most uncommon fault), both of which you will charitably impute to the proper cause. I will try to do better another time. Believe me to be, my dear friend, yours faithfully,

THOMAS CARLYLE.

XXIX.—To his MOTHER, Mainhill.

EDINBURGH,*Thursday, 17th December* 1818.[1]

MY DEAR MOTHER—I expected that the Carrier would have been here before this time, and that consequently I should have had it in my power to give you notice of my condition, without putting you to the expense of postage. But as there is now little probability of his arriving this week, I can no longer delay to answer the letter which I received from my Father a considerable time ago. Few things in the world could give me greater pleasure than to learn that you are all in good health, and that your affairs are in a somewhat prosperous condition. I trust they still continue so. The boys deserve my thanks for the alacrity with which they explored the condition of that same unfortunate box. I call it unfortunate, for upon calling at the person Kay's in the Grass-market here, I found it ill-used in every particular. In the first place, though the carriage,

---

[1] A few sentences from this letter are printed in Froude's *Life of Carlyle.*

as appeared by the marks upon the lid, had
been paid—the poor dog Beck had contrived to
make Kay (as a Porter testified) pay it again,
inadvertently—and *he* stoutly refused to part
with it, unless he were reimbursed. This, by
the way, was the reason why it had never come
to Kirkcaldy ; all the carriers refusing to take
it, because they must first pay the carriage to
Edinburgh, which was marked as paid already.
So the poor box was left standing for six weeks,
in a damp cellar, without any one to claim it.
I was forced to comply with Signor Kay's re-
quisition—and upon paying him the 2s. 10d.,
had my articles brought home at last. The
socks fit me well, and altogether are admirable
things. The butter also was there undamaged:
but the shirts—which your kindness had in-
cited you to make for me—those shirts I was
enraged to find all spotted and sprinkled with a
black colour—which the body Davie here says
is *mellemdew*—and which will never come out,
according to the same authority. I have had
them washed ; but the blackness remains.
Much of it is about the breast, and if it be

true that it cannot be erased, I must make
night-shirts of them.　This cannot be remedied,
and therefore ought not to be regretted; but
the creature Smith should refund his carriage-
money at the least.　I find living here very
high.　An hour ago, I paid my week's bill,
which, though 15s. 2d., was the smallest of the
three which I have yet discharged.　This is an
unreasonable sum when I consider the slender
accommodation, and the paltry ill-cooked morsel which is my daily pittance.　There is also
a schoolmaster right over my head, whose
noisy brats give me at times no small annoy-
ance.　On a given night of the week, he also
assembles a select number of vocal performers,
whose *music* (as they charitably name it) is now
and then so clamorous, that (when studying a
Mathematical theorem) I almost wished the
throats of these sweet singers full of molten
lead, or any other substance which might stop
their braying, for the time.　Yet neither can this
be avoided.　I was through about fifty rooms
the other day—only *one* was offered cheaper
and that greatly inferior—so I shall be content

till the spring.   There is nothing very tragical
in all this: yet it is the worst side of the picture.
I ought not to forget that I am more healthy
than I have been this twelvemonth.   I have
plenty of time to read, and am not destitute of
good society—that of Irving—James Brown, a
truly good lad, who was at Mainhill once—
Francis Dixon, etc.   Also I have *three hours*
of private teaching—at two guineas a month
for each hour.   The first two hours I got three
weeks ago.   A young man had been directed
to Irving to get lessons in Astronomy—Irving
not finding it convenient to supply him, sent
him to me : and I engaged immediately.   His
name is Robertson—he is an officer in the East
India Company, and I find him a pleasant youth.
I am only sorry that he must leave this place,
in a short time, and thus cut off my salary.
The other hour, which I undertook ten days
ago, is devoted to teach Geometry to an old
English (or Jersey) gentleman, called Saumarez,
who asked Irving one day in the Natural History class, which I also attend, if he could re-
commend a mathematical teacher—and was

immediately introduced to me. He is a most amusing creature, and the space between 8 and 9 o'clock which I daily spend with him—no less than the arguments we have together in the class, about Newton and natural philosophy—is often the most diverting of the day. He lives at the north end of the New Town, above a mile from this place; and this walk for me, before breakfast (which is of porridge), is another advantage. Robertson lives with his mother, much in the same quarter. I go thither between ten and twelve o'clock. Then comes a walk with Brown or Dixon—or else a bout at reading till two; next the Natural History class till three; then dinner of fish or mutton and roots;—and reading till midnight. This is a picture of my life; and notwithstanding a fair proportion of anticipations and forebodings, I am not at all uncomfortable.

I saw Professor Leslie twice or thrice since I wrote to you. He requested me to attempt a most difficult problem which he was going to put into a book that he is publishing. He had not time for it himself. I wrought at

it for a week; and, notwithstanding several
advances, could not do it. The day before
yesterday, he advised me to let it alone a while
—which I was willing to do; and then to try it
again, which I also intend to do. " Upon the
whole," said this curious philosopher, " I see
nothing so eligible for you as to learn the
engineer business; and then go *to America.*
Great business there—Swiss gentleman went
lately—making a large fortune—many bridges
and canals—I must have you introduced to
Jardine." This Jardine is an engineer of this
city; and came from Millhousebridge near
Lochmaben—report says he is a conceited dis-
agreeable person. You will start, my dear
Mother, at the sound of America. I too had
much rather live in my own country; and lay
my bones in the soil which covers those of my
Fathers. Nor do I despair of getting a comfortable situation for the exercise of my talents
somewhere within this sea-girt isle. On
Monday I received a letter from Mr. Duncan
of Ruthwell containing three notes of introduction—one to a certain Bailie Waugh, a

bookseller of this place who wishes to employ me as a writer in some *Review* which he is about to commence.   I had half an hour's pleasant chat with this Bailie, left my address with him, and went on my way.   What the upshot may be I cannot guess.   A second letter I delivered to Dr. Brewster, Editor of the *Edinburgh Encyclopædia.*[1]   He received me kindly—took my address—talked with me a while on several subjects—and let me go.   The kind minister of Ruthwell had, I understand, written about getting me to write in the *Encyclopædia*—the Doctor said nothing on that head.   No matter.   The third letter is to J. A. Henderson, Esq., Advocate, which I have not yet delivered.   Perhaps he will inform me about the lawyer business. This law, I sometimes think, is what I was intended for naturally.   I am afraid it takes several hundreds to become an Advocate.   But for *this*, I should commence the study of it with great hopes of success.   We shall see whether it is possible.   One of the first advocates of the

---

[1] Brewster had undertaken the editorship of the *Edinburgh Encyclopædia* in 1808 ; the work was not completed till 1830.

day, Forsyth, raised himself from being a disconsolate Preacher to his present eminence.
Therefore I entreat you, my Mother, not to
be any way uneasy about me. I see none of
my fellows with whom I am very anxious to
change places. They are mostly older than I
by several years, and have as dim prospects
generally as need be. Tell the boys to *read*,
and not to let their hearts be troubled for me.
Tell them, I am a stubborn dog—and evil fortune shall not break my heart, or bend it
either, as I hope. I must write to them and
to my Father before long.

I know not how to speak about the washing
which you offer so kindly. Surely you thought,
five years ago, that *this* troublesome washing
and baking was all over ; and *now* to recom-
mence! I can scarcely think of troubling you.
Yet the clothes are ill-washed here, and if the
box be going and coming anyway—perhaps
you could manage it.

.   .   .   .   .   .

But my paper is done. I add only, that with
a heartfelt wish for the happiness of you all, I

remain, my dear Mother, your affectionate
bairn,
THOMAS CARLYLE.

P.S.—I know not whether I mentioned that
Mr. Martin,[1] the minister of Kirkcaldy, of his
own accord, gave me at my departure a most
consolatory certificate—full of encomiums upon
talents, morals, etc., which gratified me not a
little. He was always kind to me. The
favourable opinion of such a man is worth the—
adverse votes of many ignorant persons. The
poor people of Kirkcaldy are *ill off*, I hear, for
a dominie. Charles Melville was here upon
the scent lately. There are many good men
amongst them. I wish they had a right school.

XXX.—To Mr. JAMES JOHNSTONE.

EDINBURGH, 8th January 1819.

MY DEAR JOHNSTONE—. . . I am grieved to

---

[1] The Rev. Mr. Martin's house had been hospitably open
to Irving and Carlyle while they were living at Kirkcaldy, and
Irving afterward married his eldest daughter. The minister
was "a clear-minded, brotherly, well-intentioned man."—
Reminiscences, i. 117.

see your embryo resolution of going to America.
It is always a mournful thing to leave our—
country; to a man of sensibility and reflection
it is dreadful. I speak not of that feeling which
must freeze the soul of an emigrant, when land-
ing on the quay of Boston or New York, he
reflects that the wide Atlantic is roaring between him and every heart that cares for his
fate. But to snap asunder, *for ever*, the asso-
ciations that bind us to our native soil ; to forget the Hampdens, the Sydneys, the Lockes,—
the Stewarts, the Burnses,—or to remember
them only as men of a foreign land ; to change
our ideas of human excellence ; to have our
principles, our prejudices supplanted ; to endure
the rubs which hard unkindness will have in
store for us ; to throw aside old friendships, and
with a seared heart to seek for new ones—all
this is terrible. And after all what would you
do there ? To teach is misery in the old world
or the new: and perhaps (if it *must* be so)
England is as fair a field for it as the Union.
I entreat you, my dear friend, to lay aside this
enterprise—at least for the present. I look

upon emigration as a fearful destiny—Not more fearful, I grant, than others that might be imagined; than such failure, for instance, as might call forth the pity of those who love us (I was about to add—and the triumph of those who hate us : but it is a paltry sentiment to care for *that ;*—if it exists within me I would wish to hide it both from you and myself); but thank Heaven things are not yet come to this. Consider the talents you possess—the classical, scientific, historical, above all, the agricultural knowledge, which you have acquired; look around you ; continue to improve your mind in patience, and do not *yet* imagine that, in our own country the gates of preferment are shut against you.   It will give satisfaction to me, and perhaps some relief to your own mind, to have your situation and views distinctly explained in your next letter.   Write to me without reserve—as to one who can be indifferent to nothing which concerns you.

It is superfluous to say that I have bid farewell to Fife.   My resolution was taken without advice, because none was to be had ; but not

without long and serious meditation. I could
not leave Kirkcaldy but with regret. There
are in it many persons of a respectable—several
of an exemplary character ; and had the tie
which united us been of a less irritating nature,
my time might have been spent very happily
among them. At present my prospects are as—
dim, and my feelings of course nearly as uncomfortable as they have been at any period
of my life. About the end of 1816, I remember—
informing you, that, in the space of two years,
my views of human life had considerably
altered. A similar period has again elapsed
and brought with it a change less marked
indeed, but not less real. Till not very long
ago, I imagined my whole duty to consist in
thinking and endeavouring. It now appears—
that I ought not only to suffer but to act. Connected with mankind by sympathies and wants
which experience never ceases to reveal, I now
begin to perceive that it is impossible to attain
the solitary happiness of the Stoic—and hurtful
if it were possible.[1] How far the creed of—

[1] *Rien ne doit tant diminuer la satisfaction que nous avons*

Epictetus may require to be modified, it is not easy to determine ; that it is defective seems pretty evident.   I quit the stubborn dogma, with a regret heightened almost to remorse ; and feel it to be a desire rather than a duty to mingle in the busy current which is flowing past me, and to act my part before the not distant day arrive, when they who seek me shall not find me.   *What* part I shall act is still a mystery. . . . Your faithful friend,

THOMAS CARLYLE.

P.S.—I forgot to say (what was indeed of no consequence) that I spent, along with Irving, the Christmas holidays in Fife.   They were the happiest, for many reasons which I cannot at this time explain, that for a long space have marked the tenor of my life.

XXXI.—To Mr. R. MITCHELL, Ruthwell Manse.

EDINBURGH, 15*th February* 1819.

MY DEAR FRIEND—Although well aware of

de nous-mêmes, que de voir que nous désapprouvons dans un temps ce que nous approuvions dans un autre, is the unpleasant but faithful observation of La Rochefoucault.—T. C.

the propensity which exists in men to speak more about themselves than others care for hearing, yet, as you have hitherto been the participator of all my schemes, I venture to solicit your forbearance and advice, at a time when I need them as much perhaps as I have ever done.

My situation may be briefly explained. All the plans that I have formed for succeeding in any profession, have involved the idea of sub-sisting in the interim by writing; and every project of this kind which I have devised, up to the present date, has been frustrated by my inability to procure books either for criticising or consulting. I have, it is true, the privilege of appearing on the floor of the College library, to *ask* for any book,—to wait about an hour and then to find it—not in. But this is of small advantage. My private teaching came to an end about a month ago : and at this time, except a small degree of attention which I pay to the shadow rather than to the substance of Mineralogy—for which science it is perhaps less surprising than unlucky that my unsettled

condition and my indifferent state of health
have left me little enthusiasm; excepting also
a slight tincture of the German language which—
I am receiving from one Robt. Jardine of
Göttingen (or rather Applegarth), in return for
an equally slight tincture of the French which
I communicate,—there is no stated duty whatever for me to perform. The source of that
considerable quantity of comfort, which I enjoy,
in these circumstances, is twofold. First, there
is the hope of better days, which I am not yet
old and worn enough to have quite laid aside.
This cheerful feeling is combined with a portion
of the universal quality which we ourselves
name firmness, others obstinacy; the quality
which I suppose to be the fulcrum of all Stoical
philosophy; and which, when the charmer
Hope has utterly forsaken us, may afford a grim
support in the extreme of wretchedness. But
there are other emotions which, at times, arise;
when, in my solitary walks round the Meadows
or Calton Hill my mind escapes from the smoke
and tarnish of those unfortunate persons, with
whom it is too much my fortune to associate,—

emotions which if less fleeting, might constitute
a principle of action at once rational and powerful.   It is difficult to speak upon these subjects
without being ridiculous if not hypocritical.
Besides, the principles to which I allude, being
little else than a more intense perception of
certain truths universally acknowledged, to
translate them into language would degrade
them to the rank of truisms.   Therefore unwill-
ingly I leave you to conjecture.   It is probable,
however, that your good-natured imagination
might lead you to overrate my resources if I
neglected to inform you that, on the whole, my
mind is far from philosophical composure.   The
vicissitudes of our opinions do not happen with
the celerity or distinctness of an astronomical
phenomenon : but it is evident that my mind,
at the present, is undergoing sundry alterations.
When I review my past conduct it seems to
have been guided by narrow and defective
views, and (worst of all) by lurking, deeply-
lurking affectation.   I could have defended
these views by the most paramount logic : but
what logic can withstand Experience ?   This is

not the first, and, if I live long, it will not be the last of my revolutions.   Thus—*velut unda supervenit undam*—error succeeds to error ; and thus while I seek a rule of life—life itself is fast flying away.   At the last, perhaps my creed may be found to resemble too nearly the memorable Tristrapedia of Walter Shandy, of which the minute and indubitable directions for Tristram's baby-clothes were finished when Tristram was in breeches.

But I forget the aphorism with which I began my letter.   Here, at least, let me conclude this long-winded account of my affairs ; and request from you as particular an account of your own.   We cannot help one another, my friend, but mutual advice and encouragement may easily be given and thankfully received. Will you go to Liverpool or Bristol or any-whither, and institute a " classico-mathematical Academy " ? or what say you to that asylum or rather hiding-place for poverty and discontent, America ?   To be fabricating lock No. 8, among the passes of the Alleghany !

Some nights ago, by the kindness of Dr.

Brewster, I was present at a meeting of the
Royal Society. It is pleasant to see persons
met together—when their object even *professes*
to be the pursuit of knowledge. But if any one
should expect to find, in George Street, an
image of the first Royal Society,—when Newton
was in the chair, and Halley at the table,—he
cannot (unless his fancy be the stronger) fail of
disappointment. He will find indeed a number
of clean, well-dressed (some of them able-bodied)
men : but in place of witnessing the invention
of fluxions or the discovery of gravitation, he
may chance to learn the dimensions of a fossil
stick, or hear it decided that a certain little
crumb of stone is neither to be called *mesotype*
nor *stilbite*. This (a critic would say) has very
much the look of drivelling. But *pauca verba.*
—Dr. B. is said to be almost the only efficient
member of this philosophical guild. I may
mention (though this has nothing earthly to do
with it) that I have seen the Doctor twice since
my first visit ; that I have met with a kind
reception, and found instruction as well as
entertainment in his conversation.

In conformity with ancient custom, I ought now to transmit you some of my studies. But I have too much conscience to dilate upon this subject. Besides, it is not so easy to criticise the brilliant work of Madame de Staël—*Considerations sur quelques Événemens de là Révolution*— as to tell you, what I learnt from a small Genevese attending Jameson's class, that she was very ugly and very immoral—yet had fine eyes, and was very kind to the poor people of Coppet and the environs. But she is gone; and with all her faults she possessed the loftiest soul of any female of her time. Upon the same authority, I inform you that Horace Benedict Saussure (whose beautiful *Voyages dans les Alpes* I have not yet finished) died twenty years ago; but Theodore, his son, is still living. Moreover Sismondi (another member of the Geneva Academy) is *un petit homme, vieux, mais vif, très vif.* I read Bailly's *Memoires d'un Témoin de la Révolution*, with little comfort. The book is not ill-written: but it grieved me to see the august historian of astronomy, the intimate of Kepler, Galileo,

and Newton, "thrown into tumult, raptured, or
alarmed," at the approbation or the blame of
Parisian tradesmen — not to speak of the
"*pauvres ouvriers*," as he fondly names the
dogs *du faubourg St. Antoine*. With regard
to Mineralogy—the maxim of Corporal Nym
is again applicable. Peace be to Brochant,
Brongniart, and "the illustrious Werner!" It
is a mournful study—and the Teacher, "a
cold long-winded native of the deep." Do
you wish to know the important fact, that the
stone which I brought from Helvellyn is feld-
spar-porphyry? Skiddaw is of *Thonschiefer*
(clay-schistus); and I firmly believe that the
other rocks of that wild country have names
equally beautiful and descriptive. Of their
properties I am forbid to know anything. *En-
veut-on la cause?* The "external characters"
are reckoned enough in the school of Freyberg.

Upon a cool comparison of dates, I find that
if I carry this letter to the post-office to-night,
you may have it on Monday. The thing is
then resolved upon. But it verges upon midnight; and it is high time to conclude the

useless labours of the day—on which I have
walked to Dalkeith for the purpose of exercise,
—heard a heart-rending sermon—and have
not studied the moon's erection in *Lalande.*
When am I to hope for an answer? It may
be short or long—it will not fail to comfort the
soul of, my dear Mitchell, your faithful friend,

THOMAS CARLYLE.

XXXII.—From his FATHER.

MAINHILL, 20*th February* 1819.

DEAR SON—We received the box with your
letters in it, which we were very glad to see,
and you said it was a long time since you had
a letter from your Mother or me, as Sandy has
been much engaged this week and the waffler [1]
did not get his cart home till Monday, and
Sandy set out for Dumfries Fair on Tuesday
morning, and did not come home till Thursday
night, and on Friday night he was at the
library, as their Books was come home, and he
got *Guy Mannering* for the first, and we think
in time there will be a good library; however

---

[1] The carrier's nickname, whiffler, loiterer.

that may be, I thought I would send you a scrawl. I have nothing to write you worth reading, but I thought you would be disappointed if you got the box and no letter in it, but I can say we are all in good health at present. Your Mother is hearty, and baking you two or three cakes and sorting your shirts and stockings, and in short we are very comfortable, having plenty. of meal and potatoes. We have a good deal of corn this year, more than we had last year, and I think we will can pay the Rent this year at any time we think proper. We are well forward with ploughing, as there has been very little frost to stop the Ploughs this winter. . . . I must have done, but not without telling you that the little Lassies are all running about, and Jamie and John are a good deal bigger since you saw them, and Sandy and your Mother agree very well now, though we have many arguments about Religion, but none in ill-nature ; but I add no more, but all the family's kind respects to you, and I remain, dear Son, your affectionate and loving Father,

JAS. CARLYLE.

XXXIII.—To ALEXANDER CARLYLE, Mainhill.

EDINBURGH, 23d *February* 1819.[1]
(Mrs. Scott's, 15 Carnegie Street.)

MY DEAR BROTHER—I sit down to write a letter to you, at this late hour of the night, in order to inform you of some steps which I have taken since you last heard from me. The uncomfortableness of the person Davie's lodging has been frequently alluded to in our correspondence. Vermin of various sorts, which haunted the beds of that unfortunate woman, together with sluttishness and a lying, thievish, disposition with which she was afflicted—at length became intolerable ; and on Wednesday, I told the creature that her "ticket-board" (fatal signal !) must once more be hoisted—in plain words, that I was about to forsake her house entirely. She received the news with considerable dudgeon ; but as my words to her were calm and few as well as emphatic, she made no remonstrance. To secure another room was

---

[1] A brief extract from this letter is given by Mr. Froude in his *Life*.

my next care. John Forrest's place, which has few recommendations except the excellent demeanour of Mrs. F., was engaged, I found, till the beginning of April. Of the other places at which I called, some were dirty, others dear, others had a suspicious look ; none were suitable. In short, not to trouble you with the detail of these pitiful affairs, I saw no better plan than to propose a junction with one Hill (a Nephew of Mrs. Irving's—Bogside—from Panteth Hill, Mouswald), who is here studying law. He is a harmless kind of youth—and had a clean landlady, who kept two rooms with a bed in each, which we could get for 8s. per week. My proposal was immediately accepted of : and I removed hither yesterday (Monday) evening. This comradeship is not altogether to my liking, as I fear it may encumber my researches ; but when I consider the saving of 3s. 6d. per week (not to speak of that which arises from *two* eating together)—as well as the neatness and comfort which seems to pervade this place, I am induced to put up with the other inconveniences till April, when I may take Forrest's room, or have a choice of others. Besides, we stipulated to have a fire in each room when we liked at night, so that I can retire to this small chamber whenever I have anything particular to investigate. The chamber, to say truth, is not many square feet in extent, yet it will do excellently well for the short season during which I shall occupy it. *Flitting* is an operation which has, of late years, become very irksome to me ; so you are not to expect that, in this letter, I can give you any very interesting remarks : forasmuch as I have even now scarcely ended the arrangement of my goods. I write principally to send you my address, and to request an answer from some of you.

I know it will please you all to hear that my health is good. Whenever the morning is fair, I walk before breakfast ; and after finishing the German at eleven o'clock, I generally stroll for an hour or so about the environs of this city— a practice which, I know well, is the only plan for securing vigorous health. There is a young man, Ferguson (a cousin of the Celt Maclaren,

whom you dined with at Dysart),[1] formerly
Irving's assistant at Kirkcaldy—who, being
disengaged at that hour, is as glad as I to
escape from the sin and sea-coal of Edinburgh,—
and often accompanies me. He is a sensible,
pleasant man, three or four years older than
myself. On Tuesday last, when he and I were
returning into the town from our excursion, we
met Dr. Brewster, in company with two men of
note. The Doctor stopped to tell me that he
had got a paper on Chemistry written (in French)
by Berzelius, professor of that science at Stock-
holm—which was to be published in April :—
would I translate it ? I answered in the affir-
mative ; and next day went over to get the
paper in question. It consists of six long sheets,
written in a cramp hand, and in a very diffuse
style. I have it more than half-done. The
labour of writing it down is the principal one.
In other respects there is no difficulty. I
do not expect great remuneration for this thing;
but as I am anxious to do it pretty well, it inter-
rupts my other pursuits a little. Before I began

[1] A village near Kirkcaldy, now almost joined to it.

it, I was busied in preparing to write about—
some other thing; but what will be the upshot
of it I cannot say. I tell you all these things,
because I know that nothing which concerns
me is matter of indifference to you.

About a week ago, I very briefly discussed
an *hour* of private teaching. A man in the
New Town applied to one Nicol, public teacher
of Mathematics here, for a person to give instruction in Arithmetic or something of that
sort. Nicol spoke of me, and I was in consequence directed to call upon the man next
morning. I went at the appointed hour, and
after waiting a few minutes, was met by a stout
impudent-looking man—with red whiskers—
having very much the air of an attorney, or
some creature of that sort. As our conversation may give you some insight into these
matters, I report the substance of it. " I am
here," I said after making a slight bow, which
was just perceptibly returned, " by the request
of Mr. Nicol to speak with you, sir, about a
mathematical teacher whom he tells me you
want." " Aye. What are your terms ?" " Two

guineas a month, for each hour." "*Two guineas!!*
for private *teaching*—that is perfectly extrava-
gant!" "I *believe* it to be the rate at which
every teacher of respectability in Edinburgh
officiates ; and I *know* it to be the rate below
which *I* never officiate." "*That* won't *do* for
my friend." "I am sorry that nothing less will
do for *me*. Good morning." And I retired
with considerable deliberation. The time has
been when I should have vapoured not a little,
at being so cavalierly treated by a wretched
person of this description. But it is altered
now. I reflected only that this man wanted
(and that was natural) to have his business done
cheap ; and that his ill-breeding was his mis-
fortune perhaps as much as crime. A day may
come when I shall look back upon these things
with a smile,—if that day should never come,
the maxim of the poet is not more trite than
true—

"Honour and shame from no condition rise ;
Act *well your part: there* all the honour lies."   —

This world, my boy, is but a fight at best ;
and though the battle go against us, yet he—

who quits him like a man is an object upon which (as an old philosopher has written) superior natures delight to look.

Last week I received an umbrella which I had left in Fife, and a kind letter from Mr. Swan. If ever I come to anything, *that* is one person whom I shall remember.

.   .   .   .   .   .

Tell me how Father, Mother, and all the rest of you are doing. Give my kindest love to all about the house, and believe me to be, my dear Brother, yours faithfully,

Thomas Carlyle.

XXXIV.—From his Mother and his Sister Margaret.

Mainhill, 25*th March* 1819.

Dear Tom—It is a long time since I wrote you a single line, and I am blundering already, as I am very desirous to know how you are coming on. Tell me all about it. Do you sit late? Do you read a Chapter or two every night? I hope you do, and pray for a blessing on all your undertakings. O seek while you have time to know Him whom to know is life eternal ; our time is short and also uncertain. I am sorry to inform you that my sister Mary died last Sabbath night. We must all follow in a little, and O that we were wise to think on our latter end. I beg, Tom, you do not sit late to injure your health ; but I will say no more, but hope you will excuse this scrawl, and I am, your affectionate Mother,   PEGGY C.

MY DEAR BROTHER—We received your letter, and we were very happy to hear that you were in good health. There is nothing that is worth telling you about. I have read *Guy Mannering*, and I liked it very well. I have read the *Indian Cottage*, and I liked it very much. I am reading the *History of England*, and I have got to the reign of George III. I will have done, as Sandy has to go to the clachan[1] this night. I add no more, but that I remain your

MARGARET CARLYLE.

[1] Village.

XXXV.—To ALEXANDER CARLYLE, Mainhill.

EDINBURGH, 29*th March* 1819.

My DEAR BROTHER—I snatch a hurried hour from the German lesson, to answer your kind and entertaining epistle, which reached me this forenoon. I need not say how pleasing it is to me to learn that you are all in good bodily health and comfortable spirits. The most important part of my task will be accomplished, when I have assured you that the same is the case with me. I still walk out before breakfast— and for an hour or two after ; of which practice I find the beneficial effects in an increased appetite for *victual*, and a general vigour of body. I have no doubt that two or three months of summer exercise will completely restore this my *digestive apparatus* (as our Professor calls it) to that state of activity which a person at my age, not addicted to excesses of any kind, and gifted with a sound constitution, ought naturally to expect. . . .

I am glad to understand that the library is in a prosperous state. It is to be hoped that our native village will no longer be the scorn of neighbouring districts, for its deficiency in this particular.

You are very right in stating that the Abbé Raynal is rash in some of his conjectures.— He was a jesuit priest in his time; but afterwards quarrelled with them—renounced their society, and with it, all moderation in treating of their religion. He was obliged to leave France for his opinions, and resided for a time in England, and lastly in the Netherlands. The man seems to have had a fiery temper; and it is only for the *facts* that his books contain, that any one can respect them. There is no wonder that you feel it impossible to find much time for reading in the present season. Keep doing a little at your hours of relaxation —both in writing and reading; and you will never repent it. In reading Raynal, you will, of course, attend to the Geography of the countries.

What ails that indolent young person, Doil, or more properly speaking, Jack, that he will not write? If I had any time, I would send him a letter this very night.

With respect to my occupations at this period; they are not of the most important nature. Berzelius' paper is printed. I was this day correcting the proof-sheet. The translation looks not very ill in print. I wish I had plenty more of a similar kind to translate: and good pay for doing it. Let us wait a while. I am still at the German, as I hinted above. My teacher is not a man (any more than he was a boy) of brilliant parts; but we go on in a loving way together—and he gives me the *pronunciation* correctly, I suppose; I am able to read books, now, with a dictionary. At present I am reading a stupid play of Kotzebue's—but to-night I am to have the history of Frederick the Great from Irving. I will make an *awfu' struggle* to read a good deal of it and of the Italian in summer—when at home. . . .

There is nothing new here that I wot of— fierce sort of weather, which I daresay is no stranger to you. How do the farming operations proceed? I hope to help you at the hay-time. But time is our tedious scroll should now have ending. I am always, my dear Boy, yours faithfully,

THOMAS CARLYLE.

XXXVI.—To his MOTHER, Mainhill.

EDINBURGH, *Monday* (*29th March*), 1819.[1]

MY DEAR MOTHER—I am so much obliged to you for the affectionate concern which you express for me in that brief letter—that I cannot delay to send you a few words by way of reply.[2] I need not repeat what I have already told to Sandy, who will be glad to communicate it, that I am in good health. If I continue to walk, I shall become very strong shortly. I was affected by the short notice you give me of Aunt Mary's death, and the short reflection with which you close it. It is true, my dear Mother, that "we must all soon follow her"— such is the unalterable and not unpleasing doom

[1] The larger part of this interesting letter is given by Mr. Froude, *Life*, i. 62.

[2] Mr. Froude prints this sentence as follows: "I am so much obliged to you for the affectionate concern which you express for me in that long letter, that I cannot delay to send you a few brief words by way of reply."

of men—then it is well for those who, at that awful moment which is before every one, shall be able to look back with calmness, and forward with hope. But I need not dwell upon this solemn subject—it is familiar to the thoughts of every one who has any thought.

I am rather afraid that I have not been quite regular in reading that best of books which you recommended to me. However, last night I was reading upon my favourite Job ; and I hope to do better in time to come. I entreat you to believe that I am sincerely desirous of being a good man ; and though we may differ in some few unimportant particulars, yet I firmly trust that the same Power which created us with imperfect faculties will pardon the errors of every one (and none are without them) who seeks truth and righteousness with a simple heart.

You need not fear my studying too much. In fact, my prospects are so unsettled that I do not often sit down to books with all the zeal that I am capable of. You are not to think I am fretful. I have long accustomed my mind

to look upon the future with a sedate aspect;
and, at any rate, my hopes have never yet
failed me.   A French author (D'Alembert, one—
of the few persons who deserve the honourable
epithet of honest man) whom I was lately
reading, remarks that one who devotes his
life to learning ought to carry for his motto
Liberty, Truth, Poverty; for he that fears the
latter can never have the former.   This should
not prevent one from using every honest effort
to attain a comfortable situation in life; it says
only that the best is dearly bought by base
conduct, and the worst is not worth mourning
over.   But I tire you, I doubt.   We shall
speak about all these matters more fully in
summer.   For I am meditating just now to
come down to stay awhile with you, accompanied with a cargo of books—Italian, German,
and others.   You will give me yonder little
room—and you will 'waken me every morning
about 5 or 6 o'clock—then *such* study.   I shall
delve in the yard too; and in a word become
not only the wisest but the strongest man in
those regions.   This is all *claver*, but it pleases

one. The young man Murray (with whom I used to correspond) informs me that he thinks of going to teach and preach in the island of Man : and invites me to spend a month or two with [him]. Perhaps it would be well to go. But we shall talk about all this afterwards.

If the carrier do not come before a fortnight, you may direct the box to me at Forrest's. I long to have some cakes. The last, I think, were the best I ever ate. The butter you will be astonished to learn is nearly done. I have no doubt that it has been filched : and besides Hill has eaten of it since I came, having given me meal in return. If you send any, let it be a pound or so. I am reduced to this part of the sheet [the first page, above the date] to subscribe myself, my dear Mother, yours most affectionately,
THOMAS CARLYLE.

XXXVII.—From his MOTHER.[1]

MAINHILL, 10*th April* 1819.

DEAR SON—I received your letter gladly,

1 Printed in part, and with errors, in *Life*, i. 63.

and was happy to hear of your welfare. We are all about our ordinary way, thank God!

Oh, my dear, dear son, I would pray for a blessing on your learning. I beg you with all the feeling of an affectionate mother you would study the Word of God, which He has graciously put in our hands. Oh, that it may powerfully reach our hearts, that we may discern it in its true light. God made man after His own image, therefore he behoved to be without any imperfect faculties. Beware, my dear son, of such thoughts ; let them not dwell on your mind. God forbid! But I daresay you will not can read this scrawl. I have sent you a few cakes and a little butter. I will send you more next time. Send the box back with the carrier. I would advise you to come home early in season. I know it would be for your health, and it is surely very necessary. Do send me a long letter and tell me when you will be home, and all your news. I am in a hurry, as you may see by blunders I have [made]. I hope you will overlook them, and I am [your] affectionate mother,   MARGARET CARLYLE.

P.S.—Do make religion your great study, Tom ; if you repent it, I will bear the blame for ever.

XXXVIII.—To Mr. R. MITCHELL, Ruthwell Manse.

MAINHILL, 31*st May* 1819.

MY DEAR FRIEND—In compliance with your request, I transmit to you, by the medium of our dearly beloved Johnstone, the information which I have gleaned respecting your Brother at St. John's,—and the plan of our correspondence during the summer.   It is the rainy evening of a dull day, which I have spent in reading a little of Klopstock's *Messias* (for the man— Jardine, who broke his engagement) ; and in looking over the inflated work of Squire Bristed on *America and her Resources.*[1]   "Vivacity," therefore, on my part, is quite out of the question.   But without further preface. . . .

I have done, as usual, almost nothing since

---

[1] This book, which made some noise at the time, was by the Rev. John Bristed, a clergyman of the Church of England, who settled in America.

we parted. Some one asked me with a smile, of which I knew not the meaning, if I would read *that* book, putting into my hands a volume of Rousseau's *Confessions.* It is perhaps the most remarkable tome I have ever read. Except for its occasional obscenity, I might wish to see the remainder of the book ; to try, if possible, to connect the character of Jean Jacques with my previous ideas of human nature. To say he was mad were to cut the knot without loosing it. At any rate, what could have induced any mortal, mad or wise, to recollect and delineate such a tissue of vulgar debauchery, false-heartedness and misery, is quite beyond my comprehension. If we regret our exclusion from that Gallic constellation, which has set, and found no successor to its brilliancy—the *Memoirs of Marmontel* or Rousseau's *Confessions* should teach a virtuous Briton to be content with the dull sobriety of his native country. I will not speak of the Abbé Raynal: of others I have nothing to say.

It is late ; the husbandmen of this rustic mansion are all sunk in profound repose : why should *I* longer wake ? A slender steed is to be saddled for me to-morrow by six o'clock— whereupon I design to ride with this sheet to Johnstone at Bogside—an important errand, you will say. Meanwhile, Good-night. Ever yours,

THOMAS CARLYLE.

.   .   .   .   .   .

XXXIX.—To Mr. R. MITCHELL, Ruthwell Manse.

MAINHILL, 14*th July* 1819.

I have not taken up the pen, my dear Mitchell, because of being smit with the love of sacred letter-writing ; but simply to acquit me of a debt, which for some time has lain rather heavy on my conscience. An ancient sage philosopher has said that nothing should be done *invita Minerva;* my respect for antiquity is very considerable ; but without infringing such precepts, which laziness also raises her amiable voice to applaud, my terrestrial exploits would quickly have a close. After all, this communication by letter gives occasion to many squabbles between the moral and the active

powers : I wish from my soul some less labori-
ous mode of friendly intercourse could be
devised. Much may be done in the flight of
ages. I despair of steam indeed ; notwithstanding its felicitous application to so many
useful purposes : but who can limit the undis-
covered agents with which Knowledge is yet to
enrich Philanthropy? Charming prospect for
the dull, above all, the solitary dull of future
times! Small comfort for us, however, who in
no great fraction of one age shall need to care
nothing about the matter. But wherefore
whine ? Employing rather our own very limited
gifts,. *agamus pingui Minervâ, ut aiunt*—since
we can have no other. The best quality which
I can communicate to my narrative of my
journey to Cumberland is extreme brevity. In
fact, however strongly a love of the sublime
might tempt me to renew the kind anxiety you
felt on our account, the love of truth, which is
or ought to be more powerful, compels me to
declare that nothing dangerous or wonderful
occurred. Maugre the predictions of your light-
bodied grocer, the Skinburness wherry buffeted

the billows of the Solway, as proudly as ever
the Bucentaur did those of the unquiet Adriatic.
We had not even the dubious pleasure of being
frightened. A poor Cumbrian statesman, however, enjoyed a more spirit-stirring fortune.
Unused to his situation, he cast a penetrating
glance upon "the secrets of the hoary deep;"
his visage became pallid and elongated; and
when, turning round, he noticed the entrance of
a spoonful of spray—"*Lock*," he exclaimed in
a sepulchral tone, "*Lock prasarve us ! see as
it's coomin' jain' in theare !*"[1] But the lapse of
two hours delivered him from all his terrors.
On arriving at Workington next morning, the
Severn, we were told, was not to proceed on
her voyage for a week. Though wishing to
enjoy the melancholy satisfaction of seeing
Johnstone fairly under way;[2] yet, when Friday

[1] See how it is coming rushing in there.

[2] Mr. Johnstone was about to sail for Nova Scotia, where,
at Annapolis Royal, he was to be tutor in the family of a Mr.
Ritchie. Mitchell, in a letter of 23d April 1819 says,
"Johnstone would rival Moses if he were living, being by far
the meekest man in these times. Like Kilmeny, he is as pure
as pure can be ; like Nicodemus [*sic*] he is one in whom there
is no guile."

came, and (Harrington, Whitehaven, Cocker-
mouth, Crummock Water, etc., being visited)
his day of sailing was still at a considerable
distance—the opportunity of a Dumfries sloop
induced me to take farewell of our friendly
emigrant. What my feelings were that afternoon, I need not describe. To some days of
mournful excitement, a sort of stupor had succeeded, which the noise of two half-civilised
shipmen and the task of *guessing* at some
stanzas of Tasso were little calculated to dispel.
By this time, poor James is most probably in-
specting the rugged shores of Fundy Bay. Let
us hope that his talents, and those virtues which
are their modest adornment, will secure, from
the Acadians, that affection and esteem which
all who know him have never failed to pay. I
do not wish you to convince me that we three
shall never meet again under more benign
auspices.

Since my return, except one journey to
Dumfries, which I undertook for the purpose of
engaging a supply of poetry, reviews, and such
small gear, during my continuance in these

parts,—I have not been four miles from home. Jardine gives me a solitary lesson each week in German, which I repay by one in French. Of Italian nothing should be said : and with respect to Lesage's *Theory of Attraction*,[1] my efforts are feeble and far between. I know not if there be a Goddess of Sloth—though considering that this of all our passions is the least turbulent and most victorious, it could not without partiality be left destitute. But if there be, she certainly looks on with an approving smile—when in a supine posture I lie for hours with my eyes fixed upon the pages of Lady Morgan's *France* or the travels of Faujas de Saint-Fond[2]—my mind seldom taking the pains even to execrate the imbecile materialism, the tawdry gossiping of the former, or to pity the infirm speculations and the already antiquated Mineralogy of the latter. What shall I say to the woebegone Roderick, last of the Goths; and others of a similar stamp? They

[1] Lesage's *Traité de Physique Mécanique* was published in 1818.

[2] Probably *Voyage en Angleterre, en Écosse et aux îles Hébrides*, par Faujas de Saint-Fond, Paris, 1797.

go through my brain as light goes through an achromatic telescope. When even this task becomes tiresome; or when the need of exercise (which I never neglect for a day with impunity) induces me to take the fields; I saunter about, building deceitful hopes; or when otherwise disposed, indulging an obdured recklessness, which I am apt enough to dignify with the name of patience. Do you know of a more edifying life? Seriously it becomes you, as my Father Confessor, to administer an appropriate rebuke.

I am glad to hear of your innocent enjoyments. ˙Malcolm Laing produced in me, some years since, an opinion of Ossian similar to yours;[1] from which indeed I do not recollect of hearing any but one person dissent. The

[1] "I have just been reading," Mitchell had written in his last letter, "Malcolm Laing's dissertation on the authenticity of Ossian's Poems, which seems to prove beyond the possibility of a doubt that these productions existed nowhere but in the brain of the Schoolmaster of Badenoch. M'Pherson's life in his Son-in-law's [Dr. Brewster's] *Encyclopædia* gives us to understand nearly the same thing, and I confess to you that I feel a sort of secret pleasure in beholding lying vanities like these exposed to public indignation and contempt. I would be glad to know your opinion on this subject."

exception in question was an Aboriginal from
the edge of Mid-Lorn, whom I met with last
Winter. Some two hundred Latin vocables,
which he had picked up at St. Andrews, seemed
only to have strengthened his conviction of the
Gael's infinite superiority in every department
of Nature and Art. The mention of the sledge-
cars, the itch, the ignorance of his Celtic kins-
men was a piercing thrust, which could not be
parried by the barrenness and altitude of the
highland hills, since Switzerland was ready
with her Alps to oppose his Grampians, and
with her Zwingles, her Gessners, her Hallers,
Eulers, Bernouillis, to eclipse his solitary Fergusson and Maclaurin. Poor Pseudo-Ossian
was silenced as easily by the intrepid Orkney
man ; and this fervid patriot, after an hour of
torture, uttered a keen vituperation on Malcolm
and me for being " Mongrels of the plain,"
which shut the scene. " The schoolmaster of
Badenoch," like every dog, has had his day.

You speak very much at your ease about
visiting me in—a few weeks ! I should lose
patience, but there is one sad and sole relief—

if the mountain will not come to Mahomet,
Mahomet knows what course to take. I was
going to say one of these Saturdays, but, since
I began to write, a letter from Dr. Brewster
has arrived, which will very possibly bring me
over on Saturday first. It is about that cal-
culating Geo. Ross ; and I must see Mr.
Duncan. The letter has already spent a week
upon the road, and there is no time to lose.
Expect me therefore, unless "Diana in the
shape of rain "¹ prevent me and my poor shelty
from travelling. O! that I saw the "imp of
fame" wherewith poor Murray is in travail!

---

¹ The allusion to "Diana" as an obstruction in one shape
or another, was one that Carlyle made more than once in later
years. See his letter to Emerson of 13th May 1835, and his
letter to me in 1874, cited in a note to the letter to Emerson
in the published Correspondence of Carlyle and Emerson,
i. 69. But his memory, usually of extraordinary accuracy,
had in this, through all his life, played him false. The allusion was derived from *Hudibras*. But in *Hudibras* it is
" Pallas," not "Diana," who intervenes to hinder the intent
of the knight.

> '' But Pallas came in shape of rust,
> And 'twixt the spring and hammer thrust
> Her Gorgon shield, which made the cock
> Stand stiff, as 'twere transform'd to stock.''
>   *Hudibras*, Part i. Canto ii. 781-784.

"The Stewartry."[1]   But I have done.—Yours, my dear Mitchell, in all sincerity of heart,

THOMAS CARLYLE.

XL.—To JOHN A. CARLYLE, Mainhill.

EDINBURGH, 11*th November* 1819.

MY DEAR BROTHER—At length I have leisure to devote a few minutes to the duty of detailing the particulars of my history, since our parting on the summit of Ericstane. . . .

I am seated in the back-room of a Mrs. Thomson (wife of a Tailor), which I rent at the rate of 6s. per week, fire included. This person seems to have a good character in the neighbourhood; and from the few symptoms I have yet been able to observe, it appears likely that I shall be very snug here. The room is not large, but it is clean,—and the neat little landlady says it is perfectly free of smoke and of most detested *bugs*.

---

[1] The Stewartry of Kirkcudbright. This, in reference to Murray's *Literary History of Galloway*, published in 1822: "valuable but undeservedly neglected," Lowndes calls it.

Thus, my dear Jack, have I written for thy friendly perusal a full account of my transactions up to this date. The Waffler (well he deserves that *nom de guerre!*) is not yet come to town; so that being unable to transact any business, I have full leisure to reflect upon every part of my condition. Pretty strong in body, and capable, as I know, of vigorous effort, I am far from despairing. However, as I have nothing new to tell you upon this subject, I forbear to discuss it further for the present. Let us be contented, my bonny boy, prudent, active, resolute in improving *every* advantage which our situation affords—and moderate success is hardly doubtful.

9 o'clock P.M.—After an interval of five hours, spent in reading the *Edinburgh Review*, and executing various commissions, I resume my lucubrations. The unhappy carrier is not come. What can it be that keeps him? Is his steed foundered—or himself overpowered with liquor? Alas! poor Rose!

At this time, I guess, Alick and the rest of

you are seated around the *room*-fire—each pursuing his respective study. Good luck to you all! Be diligent and you will not miss your reward. Tell the small *childer* that I expect copies from them all, next box,—letters from all that have *any* powers of diction, and have advanced beyond the *strokes* in the art of writing.

Having scarcely spoken to any one since my arrival, I have none of that much-coveted commodity, news, to send you. The burghers of this city are, for most part, minding their private affairs ; and the few of them who take any share in public transactions, are occupied, as elsewhere, in talking about the massacre of Manchester, and the foolish Carlile's conduct at his trial. The distress under which the universal kingdom suffers seems not to be felt in Edinburgh—to the extent that it is likely ere long to reach. Already, however, there is much poverty among the lowest orders ; and the issue of this crisis seems anxiously anticipated by all. For the rest, *dandies* and cattle of that stamp are still in considerable force ;

but you and I have other things to do than take up our time with them.

Have you got Hume yet? Does Geo. Johnston come to get his French lesson from you? Try the Latin, if he come : you are sure to make progress in it ; most probably it will turn to good account for you, and any way, it is a wholesome adage that says : Can do is easily carried about with one. Again let me renew my often repeated desire that you will punctually attend to your writing. I must send you *lines* —unless I forget—as I did to give you the money last Tuesday 'till I was several miles from you, when it was utterly useless to deplore my negligence. Send me your copy to inspect any way. I finish, my dear Jack, with sub-scribing myself, thy affectionate brother,

THOMAS CARLYLE.

XLI.—To Mr. R. MITCHELL, Ruthwell Manse.

EDINBURGH, 18*th November* 1819.

MY DEAR MITCHELL—Without reluctance, I push aside the massy quarto of Millar on the

English government,[1] to perform the more
pleasing duty of writing a few lines to you, by
the conveyance of Mr. Duncan. No material
event has been added to my history since the
day when I parted with you at the avenue of
Cummertrees : but by scribbling upon some
portion of this sheet, I expect to secure the
advantage of hearing from you in return ; and
independently of this, if my labour do no good,
the comfort is, it can do little ill.

I reached what certain persons have been
pleased to call "the intellectual city," on the
afternoon of yesterday-week. The country of
Tweedsmuir, you have often heard me say, is
the most mournful in Europe. Rugged, without being elevated ; barren, stormy, and covered,
at least in winter, with an ever-brooding darkness, it seems a fit haunt for the harassed
fanatics who tenanted it in the seventeenth
century. I never crossed this dismal region
without melancholy, bitter recollections of the

---

[1] The once noted book of Professor John Millar of Glasgow, entitled *An Historical View of the English Government*,
first published in 1787.

good which I had left ; and forebodings of the
evil I was likely to meet with : in short, if
Trophonius should ever think of setting up in
the world again, I would have him leave far
behind the vales of Thessaly, however tempt-
ing they may seem, and dig his grotto in some
hope[1] of this dark Cimmerian desert! You may
wonder why I so vehemently abuse this "excellent sheep country :." I cannot say—unless
that on Tuesday the roads were very bad and
the weather very wet; and according to David
Hume *contiguity in time or place* is a principle
of association among our ideas.

Since my arrival in Edinburgh, the employment of waiting for carriers, travelling to Fife,
etc., has consumed most of my time. On Tuesday morning the benevolent Mr. Duncan carried me to Bailie Waugh's. This worshipful
magistrate seems (under the rose) to be a very
flimsy vapouring sort of character. I left him
my address ; and shall probably hear no. more
of him. With regard to your most kind Minister, my circumstances qualify me but poorly

[1] *Hope* = a sloping hollow between two hills.

for doing any justice to the feelings which his
conduct is calculated to excite. Even to you
I cannot enter upon this subject. Yester-night
I enrolled in the class of Scots law.[1]   The Professor, Dr. Hume, a nephew of the philosopher
already mentioned, speaks in a voice scarce
audible ; and his thinking has yet to show all
its points of similarity with the penetrating
genius of his Uncle. Yet I prophesy I shall
not dislike the science. If health continue, I
shall feel for it all the ardour which is naturally
inspired by the prospect (however dubious) of its
affording a permanent direction to my efforts : I
shall require, moreover, to investigate the history,
antiquities, manners, etc., of our native country
—a subject for which I feel nothing like repugnance : and for the details of the subject—six

[1] " I had thought of attempting to become an advocate. It
seemed glorious to me for its independency, and I did read some
law books, attend Hume's lectures on Scotch law, and converse
with and question various dull people of the practical sort.
But it and they and the admired lecturing Hume himself appeared to me mere denizens of the kingdom of dulness, point-
ing towards nothing but money as wages for all that bogpool
of disgust. Hume's lectures once done with, I flung the thing
away for ever."—Note of Carlyle's cited by Froude in his *Life
of Carlyle*, i. 64.

years of solitary reading (would it had been *study !*) have given me a most courageous indifference to the *magnitude* of any folio capable of being lifted without the aid of the mechanical powers. My fear at the present is even that I shall *not* be able to procure a copy of Erskine's *Institutes.*[1] But next time I write you shall know more particularly about these affairs.

I have not seen Dr. Brewster, because he was not in town till this day. His journal[2] appears to be in a sickly state. Few speak of it ; and those few without respect.

There is little that I can tell you respecting the news civil or literary of these parts, which Mr. Duncan will not be much better qualified to lay before you. I heard Leslie once only. Desirous, it would appear, of beating Chalmers on his own ground, he is said to have been greatly distinguished this season for the *piety* of his opening lectures. When I was there, he spoke of many philosophers and their deeds

[1] *Institutes of the Laws of Scotland,* by John Erskine, Professor of Scottish Law in the University of Edinburgh, 1773.

[2] *The Edinburgh Philosophical Journal,* the publication of which had just begun.

from Hipparchus to Malus inclusive, in a pompous style—somewhat in Gibbon's vein—except that Gibbon is seldom tawdry. Wallace,[1] whom I went this day to see, is a person about fifty years old—short, bald-headed, with a grim and intelligent countenance. His manner is blunt; he speaks with a Scotch accent;—and if his unaffected and patient demeanour is accompanied with a display of philosophical reflection —which I cannot assert or deny—he ought surely to be a great favourite with the public. Leslie and he are said to be on the eve of battle, —for the Elements of Geometry and curves of the second order are to be discarded for Playfair's Euclid! Love me, love my dog—the saw says: still more should it say, love me, love my book. Science you see, as well as religion, is at times disturbed by the feuds of its professors. What have we to say but wish these worthies a fair field and no favour?

Non nostrum inter vos tantas componere lites:
Et vitula tu dignus, et hic.

---

[1] Professor William Wallace, appointed in 1819 Professor of Mathematics in the University of Edinburgh.

But I must quit these lucubrations—tell me very soon what progress you make in Crombie; give me an order to get you Lipsius, either of the Scaligers, Casaubon, or the never-dying Ernesti, and I shall obey you with immense cheerfulness. Seriously though, I think your study of classical literature likely to benefit you. It is not enough to pursue philosophy through all her intricate recesses : we must have a trade —since we have no fortune. And although we have quitted one profession, in which many lead a tranquil, and one or two a dignified life, it may be we shall both yet have our wishes gratified. Who knows indeed but you being Professor of Humanity, I a tired *causidicus,* may delight to interrupt your evenings of literary leisure—and call to mind the days of yore ? *Espérons*, say I always ; and in the meantime, I conclude this sheet—and its most hurried contents, with subscribing myself once more, your old and faithful friend,

THOMAS CARLYLE.

Lipsius is here—I mean his *Roma Antiqua.*

You shall have it in summer—sooner if you like. Write immediately.

XLII.—To JOHN A. CARLYLE, Mainhill.

EDINBURGH, DUFF'S LODGINGS,
35 BRISTO STREET, 2d *December* 1819.

MY DEAR JACK—I am very much satisfied, as may well be supposed, to hear that thou and the cattle got safely home—though faint, yet persevering. I have only to hope that nothing sustained any serious injury by that adventure. Most probably you are already come home from Cumberland. I trust you and our cousin (to whom give my best love) were pleased with the beautiful, though at this season prostrate, aspect of that interesting county. You have no doubt resumed your occupations; and at this hour (six o'clock) I suppose are "forming the circle" around your cheerful fire, to teach, and to be taught. Innocent group! peace be with you all!

.   .   .   .   .   .

I have very little time to enter into particulars about my studies, which indeed are yet (alas!) hardly begun. I am at the Scots law class; and the professor (a nephew of the historian Hume) is most perspicuous; but law is to me an untrodden path, and much toil will be requisite for mastering it. Yet I fear *that* little. I have got four very ponderous quartos of notes taken from these lectures, in short-hand—they promise to .be of much use to me. I have read Millar on the English govern-ment, etc. The notes came from Hill (my comrade for a part of last winter): perhaps I shall send these letters in the box, which once held these *learned* papers. But I must have done, Jack. Remember me in the most kind manner to Mag, Jemmy, Mary, Jean, and little Jenny. Tell all of them to write me that can write. Be *good* to them, poor things. Send me all your copies, write copiously (in your letter to me); and be assured that I remain, my dear Brother, yours most faithfully,

THOMAS CARLYLE.

I have not time to send the box—$7\frac{3}{4}$ o'clock.

You will send down that great ugly Italian book *Nani, Storia della Venezia,* along with the note to Annan. Geordy is to send me a book of the Scots Acts of Parliament: you will put it in the box.

XLIII.—To his MOTHER, Mainhill.

EDINBURGH, DUFF'S LODGINGS,
35 BRISTO STREET, 15*th December* 1819.

MY DEAR MOTHER—Nothing could give me greater pleasure than to learn that you continue in good health, and are improving even in that particular. I entreat you, for the sake of us all, to be careful of this invaluable privilege. It is the foundation of every earthly blessing. With it and a clear conscience, no human creature need in general be miserable. You will be satisfied to learn that I am very well. By taking a proper degree of exercise my bodily frame, I find, may be made to do its duty pretty well; and accordingly I make a point to divide the day between study and walking. It is the more necessary, as when I neglect it, the dark side of my affairs never fails to present itself to my solitary imagination, and I am as unfit for study as for flying. Upon the whole, however, I go courageously along ; and to beat the hoof half an hour before breakfast, and an hour before entering the law class at two or rather half-past one, is quite sufficient to keep me in good heart. The law I find to be a most complicated subject ; yet I like it pretty well, and feel that I shall like it better as I proceed. Its great charm in my eyes, is that no mean compliances are requisite for prospering in it. I must struggle, and solace myself with the delightful hope that the day *will* yet come when I may show you all what sense I entertain of your affectionate conduct.

The cakes are excellent and most acceptable. I think you must have left out one sock : at least I can find but three in the box. You need not take all this trouble on you, about these articles. I have plenty of socks. I know not whom to thank for the ham : doubtless it will do me good service. I have not yet fairly arranged the newspaper, not having looked for the carrier so soon. I shall tell you fully about it when he returns. Write to me very copiously, whenever you can find as much time. I trust, my dear Mother, we *shall* yet agree in all things. But absolute sameness of opinion, upon any point, is not, as I have often said, to be looked for in this low erring world. Excuse my brevity ; and believe me to be, my dear Mother, ever yours most affectionately,

THOMAS CARLYLE.

My compliments to Margaret : she must write before the milking hour another time. My father, I trust, is well, though you say nothing of him.

XLIV.—To ALEXANDER CARLYLE, Mainhill.

EDINBURGH, 15*th December* 1819.

MY DEAR ALICK— . . . You will be glad to learn that I am well and comfortable. . . . I attend the law class, with some satisfaction, and read a book called Erskine's *Institutes* upon the same. This Erskine's *Institutes* would weigh about four stones avoirdupois; and you would think the very Goddess of dulness had inspired every sentence. Yet I proceed without fainting. I go likewise occasionally to the Parliament House, and hear the pleadings. I imagine it would not be difficult to demolish certain persons whom I see gain a livelihood by pleading there. In the meantime it behoves me to live in hope, and make every effort. There is nothing new here almost. Some timorous individuals about Glasgow imagined that the Radicals (as their cant name is) intended to *rise* on Monday last; and accordingly on Saturday all the soldiers were sent from Edinburgh and Jock's Lodge;[1] our volunteers took possession of the Castle; and there was riding, running, marching, and counter-marching in every direction. I saw the yeomen set out on Sunday morning. This was very gallant; and the five thousand soldiers that surrounded Glasgow were, I doubt not, very gallant fellows; but the Radicals *stuck to their looms*. A mountain was once in labour, and when all men had

[1] Barracks in the neighbourhood.

come to see the issue—a mouse was born. So
is it with the "rebellion in the west," and the
five and twenty thousand men in arms that
were to murder all his Majesty's lieges in
Lanarkshire.[1]   I am very vexed that you see

[1] The misery of the Working Classes in England and Scotland at this period made a lasting impression on Carlyle. The
condition and disposition of these people already began to
seem to him, as he said twenty years later in his *Chartism*,
"the most ominous of all practical matters whatever." A
passage from his *Reminiscences* (i. 152) fills out the narration
in this letter.   "Year 1819 comes back into my mind as the
year of the Radical 'rising' in Glasgow; and the kind of (altogether imaginary) 'fight' they attempted on Bonnymuir against
the Yeomanry which had assembled from far and wide. A time
of great rages and absurd terrors and expectations, a very fierce
Radical and Anti-Radical time.   Edinburgh endlessly agitated
all round me by it, not to mention Glasgow in the distance;
gentry people full of zeal and foolish terror and fury, and looking disgustingly busy and important.   Courier hussars would
come in from the Glasgow region covered with mud, breathless,
for headquarters, as you took your walk in Princes Street;
and you would hear old powdered gentlemen in silver
spectacles talking with low-toned but exultant voice about
'cordon of troops, sir,' as you went along.   The mass of the
people, not the populace alone, had a quite different feeling,
as if the danger from those West-country Radicals was small or
imaginary, and their grievances dreadfully real;—which was
with emphasis my own poor private notion of it.   One bleared
Sunday morning, perhaps seven or eight A.M., I had gone out
for my walk.   At the Riding-House in Nicolson Street was a
kind of straggly group, or small crowd, with redcoats inter-

no newspaper at this most interesting period.
I must try to get a *Scotsman* some way; for I
see none myself, except when I go to the bookseller's shop, which is very unsatisfactory. You
have not sent me any copy, yet I hope you continue to write, and also to mind your spelling.
How does Hume go forward? I expect a

spersed. Coming up I perceived it was the ' Lothian Yeomanry '
(Mid or East I know not), just getting under way for Glasgow to
be part of ' the cordon.' I halted a moment. They took the
road, very ill-ranked, not numerous or very dangerous-looking
men of war ; but there rose from the little crowd, by way of
farewell cheer to them, the strangest shout I have heard
human throats utter ; not very loud, or loud even for the small
numbers ; but it said as plain as words, and with infinitely
more emphasis of sincerity, ' May the Devil go with *you*, ye
peculiarly contemptible and dead to the distresses of your
fellow - creatures ! '   Another morning, months after, spring
and sun now come, and the ' cordon,' etc., all over, I met a
gentleman, an advocate, slightly of my acquaintance, hurrying
along, musket in hand, towards the Links, there to be drilled as
an item of the ' gentlemen ' volunteers now afoot. ' You
should have the like of this,' said he, cheerily patting his
musket. ' Hm, yes ; but I haven't yet quite settled on which
side ! '—which probably he hoped was quiz, though it really
expressed my feeling.   Irving too, and all of us juniors, had
the same feeling in different intensities, and spoken only to
one another : a sense that revolt against such a load of un-
veracities, impostures, and quietly inane formalities would one
day become indispensable ;—sense which had a kind of rash,
false, and quasi-insolent joy in it ; mutiny, revolt, being a light
matter to the young."

long account of everything from you when you
write next. I do not think of leaving Edinburgh during the vacation at Christmas. I
shall stay and read or write rather. Believe
me to be, my dear Brother, yours most faithfully,

THOMAS CARLYLE.

I forgot to send your money last time. I
shall (unless this hurry mislead me) send you
four notes this journey. I believe the debt is
somewhat less, but I owe Jack something ; and
the remainder you can give my Mother for
shirts, etc., retaining a few shillings to buy me
tobacco from time to time. Keep it very wet
—the tobacco I mean.

XLV.—To ALEXANDER CARLYLE, Mainhill.

EDINBURGH, 29*th December* 1819.

MY DEAR BROTHER— . . . I said I should sfay
in Edinburgh during the Christmas holidays ;
but happily my firmness in this determination
was not put to the test. Our professor *gives no
holidays ;* so, at the present festive season, we

are labouring with our wonted assiduity in the complex study of Law. I have not yet gained much knowledge of it : but he (Mr. Hume) is very plain hitherto, and by the help of those monstrous tomes with which I am environed, there is little doubt that I may in time acquire competent information upon all the branches of this science. I have not been so diligent of late, on account of a paper I am writing—which I have a design to offer for publication. No mortal is aware of it, so you need not mention the circumstance : but I can see well enough that to this point my chief efforts should be directed. In fact, unless my pen will afford me present subsistence, what hope have I in Law ? I ought to try at least,—and I shall tell you the issue of my trial when it happens. Yet if these schemes should fail I need not still despair. Teaching and preaching are the only trades— that I have forsworn ; and it will be hard, very hard, if a humble man cannot earn his *bit of bread* in any other department of art or science. I will not despair nor even despond.

In the meantime it is pleasant to have these

few hard-earned notes by me, to answer every exigency. Economy and diligence will go far in all cases. . . . I remain, my dear Brother, yours most faithfully,   THOMAS CARLYLE.

XLVI.—To ALEXANDER CARLYLE, Mainhill.

EDINBURGH, 26th January 1820.

MY DEAR BROTHER—I was very happy to learn by the carrier's arrival, some hours ago, that you were all in a state of health and motion at the period of his departure. You will be satisfied, in your turn, to hear that I am still afoot, notwithstanding the late tremendous reign of frost, which seemed enough to destroy every symptom of animal or vegetable life. Of all the kinds of weather that in my lifetime have descended from the pitiless North, the tract which is just ended appears to have been the most appalling. What with ice and snow and biting breezes, Edinburgh seemed to be the capital of Greenland rather than of Caledonia. But the thaw has come at last, and I have gone through the process of freezing without any inconvenience, except a filthy snivelling cold, which I picked up last Saturday, and which I expect to lay down to-morrow or next day. It may last a week if it will, for it gives me very small inconvenience.

Your long letter gratified me not a little. Your are by far too severe a critic of your own productions. The account of your journey to Cumberland was replete with amusing notices. I can perfectly conceive the feelings excited by your situation at Workington, upon being re-fused admittance at Curwen's Arms. It is at such a time that the dogged stubborn sentiment of obdured patience (too nearly allied to ill-nature, in some other cases) is really valuable. One has often room to use it in the business of life. You have now partly seen Cumberland ; and though at a time of disadvantage, your journey will not be altogether fruitless : the remembrance of Skiddaw and the wild moun-tains that have frowned, since the creation's dawn, beside him, is a pleasing subject for the mind to rest on ; and even the sight of the rude but honest-hearted boors that inhabit those regions, and the comparison of their ways of thinking and acting with our own, is always attended with enjoyment, and might be with advantage.

I am truly glad to find that you persevere in Hume. The remarks you make upon the various characters of whom he treats seem just, as far as I can remember. Nor can I blame your enthusiasm at the name of Wallace or him of Bannockburn. Those heroes stood in the breach when their country was in peril; that Scotland is not as Ireland[1] is perhaps owing in a great measure to their exertions. As you proceed in the narrative, the events will become more interesting; and you will have more occasion to be on your guard against Mr. Hume's propensities to Toryism. Next time you write

[1] This thought remained with Carlyle. In *Past and Present*, published in 1843, he wrote (p. 16): "A heroic Wallace, quartered on the scaffold, cannot hinder that his Scotland become, one day, a part of England : but he does hinder that it become, on tyrannous unfair terms, a part of it. . . . If the union with England be in fact one of Scotland's chief blessings, we thank Wallace withal that it was not the chief curse. Scotland is not Ireland : no, because brave men rose there, and said, ' Behold, ye must not tread us down like slaves ; and ye shall not,—and cannot ! ' "

I shall expect to hear about Surrey and Wolsey, Elizabeth, Raleigh, Drake, etc. Before concluding, I will again take the liberty to advise you to be very careful of your writing. Your spelling is materially improved : a little further care will make it quite perfect.

Your fears about my health are very obliging ; though quite unnecessary at the present. In fact I am generally in very fair health : and I do not study at all too severely—indeed not diligently enough, I fear. For some time back I have been employed a part of each night in writing a paper for the *Edinburgh Review*. I at last gave it in last Monday—in a letter to Francis Jeffrey, Esq., desiring him to send it back if it did not suit the purpose. I have yet got no answer. Indeed, I should not be surprised if it were not accepted :[1] it was written

<hr>

[1] A fuller account of this attempt is given in the *Reminiscences* (ii. 17). " It was still some eight or ten years before any personal contact occurred between Jeffrey and me ; nor did I ever tell him what a bitter passage, known to only one party, there had been between us. It was probably in 1819 or 1820 (the coldest winter I ever knew) that I had taken a most private resolution and executed it in spite of physical and other misery, to try Jeffrey with an actual contribution to the *Edinburgh*

on a very dry subject; and I was not at the
time in my happiest mood for writing well.
But if (as is very likely) it be returned upon

Review. The idea seemed great and might be tried, though
nearly desperate. I had got hold somewhere (for even books
were all but inaccessible to me) of a foolish enough, but new
French book, a mechanical *Theory of Gravitation* elaborately
worked out by a late foolish M. Pictet (I think that was the
name) in Geneva. This I carefully read, judged of, and elaborately dictated a candid account and condemnation of, or
modestly firm contradiction of (my amanuensis, a certain feeble
but enquiring quasi-disciple of mine, called George Dalgleish of
Annan, from whom I kept my ulterior purpose quite secret).
Well do I yet remember those dreary evenings in Bristo Street;
oh, what ghastly passages and dismal successive spasms of
attempt at ' Literary Enterprise '—*Herclii Selenographia*, with
poor Horrox's *Venus in Sole visa*, intended for some ghastly
Life of the said Horrox,—this for one other instance ! I read
all Saussure's four quartos of *Travels in Switzerland* too (and
still remember much of it) I know not with what object. I
was banished, solitary, as if to the bottom of a cave, and blindly
had to try many impossible roads out ! My *review of Pictet*
all fairly written out in George Dalgleish's good clerk hand, I
penned some brief polite note to the great Editor, and walked
off with the small parcel one night to his address in George
Street. I very well remember leaving it with his valet there,
and disappearing in the night with various thoughts and doubts!
My hopes had never risen high, or in fact risen at all ; but for
a fortnight or so they did not quite die out, and then it was
absolute *zero;* no answer, no return of MS., absolutely no
notice taken, which was a form of catastrophe more complete
than even I had anticipated ! There rose in my head a
pungent little note which might be written to the great man,

me, I shall not take it greatly to heart. We can try again upon a more promising theme. No mortal but you knows of it; so I shall not feel abashed at the failure of an attempt which was honest in its nature, and will be unknown in its consequences—to any except friends. I shall tell you the result next letter. You do well to read the *Scotsman*. You will find in it a considerable quantity of information, and by combining it with the *Courier* (of the Manchester paper I know little), you will be able to

with neatly cutting considerations offered him from the small unknown ditto; but I wisely judged it was still more dignified to let the matter lie as it was, and take what I had got for my own benefit only. Nor did I ever mention it to almost anybody, least of all to Jeffrey in subsequent changed times, when at any rate it was fallen extinct. It was my second, not quite my first attempt in that fashion. Above two years before, from Kirkcaldy, I had forwarded to some magazine editor in Edinburgh what, perhaps, was a likelier little article (of descriptive tourist kind after a real tour by Yarrow country into Annandale) which also vanished without sign; not much to my regret that first one, nor indeed very much the second either (a dull affair altogether, I could not but admit), and no third adventure of the kind lay ahead for me. It must be owned my first entrances into glorious 'Literature' were abundantly stinted and pitiful; but a man does enter if, even with a small gift, he persist; and perhaps it is no disadvantage if the door be several times slammed in his face, as a preliminary."

form some idea of the state of the country,.
which at this time has an aspect particularly
striking. In case I should forget to do it elsewhere, I must beg you to tell the Sutor that I
cannot get the *Scotsman* till he send me an
order in writing to that effect. I may have it
next journey.—Believe me to be your affectionate Brother,

THOMAS CARLYLE.

XLVII.—To JOHN A. CARLYLE, Mainhill.

EDINBURGH, 26*th January* 1820.

MY DEAR JACK—I have read over your letter
with great satisfaction ; and I devote the short
while, which yet remains before Geordie's departure, to scribble this half-sheet by way of
reply to it. I ought in the first place to ask
your pardon for misdirecting you about the Latin
book you were to read. The volume in question is not, I find, at Mainhill, but here : I shall
send it down in the box, and if you can manage
it—well ; if not, send me word, and I shall not
fail to get you another edition of it, with notes

and a glossary, which you will find quite intelligible.

You do well to proceed with the Latin : it can in no case be quite useless to you ; it may eventually be of great service. The understanding of one's own Tongue is at all times an important matter ; and no way is so completely efficient for that purpose as the study of Latin, which it is mainly grounded on and derived from. But particularly attend to your penmanship ; neglect no night to write a copy—longer or shorter. I approved very much of your remarks upon David Hume. Sandy tells me that you and he are in the habit of attending chiefly to the manners, opinions and general features of the different periods which you read about. This is the true way of proceeding in the study of history. It is good, surely, because it is pleasing, to know about battles and sieges and such matters—and these things ought carefully to be stored up in the mind ; but a person who gathers *nothing more* from the annals of a nation is not much wiser than one who should treasure up the straw of a threshing-floor and leave the grain behind. You are right to attend to dates; do not neglect the geography of the countries. In a short while you will find some of your old friends whom you met with in *Charles V.* I am very glad that Alick and you are going fairly to get through Hume : it is a task which very few accomplish, notwithstanding its pleasantness and utility. No one without it can be said to understand the first principles of the laws, church government or manners of his own country. . . .

There is nothing new here ; at least nothing that penetrates my secluded abode. The common people are in great distress ; though for several reasons that distress is less severely felt here than in manufacturing districts. The substantial burghers and other idle loyalists of the place are training themselves to the use of arms for the purpose of suppressing the imaginary revolts of the lower orders. When I meet one of those heroic personages, with his buff-belts, his cartouche-box and weapons of war, obstructing the progress of his Majesty's subjects along the streets, I can scarce suppress a bitter smile

at the selfishness and stupidity of men.   In
fact "steel pills," though a very natural, are
a very ineffectual remedy for a decayed "constitution." . . .

You must write at great length next time :
send me all the news in any degree or even
no degree interesting.   Mind your reading,
that is, an account of it for my inspection.—
I am, my dear Brother, yours affectionately,

THOS. CARLYLE.

XLVIII.—To his MOTHER.

EDINBURGH, *26th January* 1820.

MY DEAR MOTHER—Though you have not
favoured me with a line this great while, yet,
as I have still a few minutes left, I take the
opportunity thus afforded me of sending you
some small account of my proceedings.

You will doubtless think me a very trust-
less person for taking no farther notice of the
Philanthropic Gazette, which I promised to
get for you.   The truth is, the poor drivelling
bookseller, about whom I spoke, hampered and

hummed so piteously last time I broached the subject, that I took compassion on his indecision and left the subject at rest. I am very sorry that you should be disappointed in this matter; but after all, I do not think very highly of the gazette in question, and the *Repository* seems to be a better book in several respects. If you want any publication that I can procure, do not fail to tell me, and it shall be forthcoming. *Anything* that I can ever do to serve you must lie far behind what I have owed to you since the earliest days of my existence.

The cakes you sent came in good season, their predecessors having been concluded two or three days ago. I was also glad to see the butter; for the first excellent pot came to an end soon after Farries' last visit to this city. The stuff which they sell here under the name of butter has few titles, often, to that honourable epithet. The main ingredient is sea-salt; the rest a yellow sour-tasted substance, which, whether it ever actually existed in the shape of milk, I cannot determine. I am likewise

obliged by the pieces of meat : but though I
have sent home the meal-poke, its contents are
not exhausted—a portion of them yet remains,
in some jar or other, for future consumption.

Having now discussed these small matters,
I must proceed to make some inquiries about
your actual situation. And first of health. I
entreat you, my dear Mother, to be careful of
that greatest of blessings. Do not expose
yourself on any account in this intemperate
weather : you are not calculated to stand it.
Indeed its effects are pernicious to any one ;
but much more to one in your situation. When
you write, I expect to hear very minutely about
every thing pertaining to you. Do you ever
recollect our evening-meals in the little room,
during the last, to me unusual but not unhappy
summer ?

I have already told the *callants*[1] that I am
in a good state of health ; therefore I need not
enlarge upon this point. My way of life is
very simple. I see few acquaintances ; those
I might see are not without good qualities, but

[1] Boys.

their conversation cannot benefit me greatly : so I devote my time to reading—all but two or three different portions of it which are daily spent in walking. Whether I shall succeed in this undertaking of law, must depend on several circumstances. Providence, as you have often told me, will regulate them. Meanwhile let no malignant person put you in fear about my future destiny. With health, which I hope to enjoy, and with a frugal disposition, which I am pretty sure of enjoying, there is no room to fear. You must write to me whenever you can find time. Remember me to my Father and all the rest about home.— I remain, my dear Mother, yours most affectionately,

THOS. CARLYLE.

XLIX.—To ALEXANDER CARLYLE, Mainhill.

EDINBURGH, 1st *March* 1820.

MY DEAR BROTHER—One of the first objects which saluted my eyes this morning, on sallying forth to take the usual walk, was the welcome figure of George Farries. But though

this diligent wayfaring man promised to send
my box to me without loss of time; and though
I did actually get it, on personal applications
being repeated, about eleven o'clock; yet so
many small engagements have intervened, that
twilight has arrived before I am able to commence my reply to your letter. . . .

I have not been altogether idle, though my
efforts have been directed to trifling objects.
The Life of Montesquieu[1] was delivered to
Brewster Saturday gone-a-week; and one of
the small engagements alluded to above, was
the concluding of Lady Mary Wortley Montagu's Life, which little George Dalgleish
finished copying for me, about an hour ago.
The two will occupy some five or six pages.
I am also to write the Life of Dr. Moore, his
son Sir John Moore, Nelson, etc. etc. I do
not get on very quickly in these operations;
but this is like my apprenticeship as it were;
in time I shall do it far more readily. So soon
as I can seize upon anything fit to be employed
with—a book to translate or the like, which I

---

[1] Job-work for the *Edinburgh Encyclopædia.*

am not altogether without hopes of doing—I shall hie to Annandale, to inhale my native breezes once again. Last summer's residence there did me a world of good : another summer so spent would entirely new-model me. If I come, I shall not fail to make proof of that *shallow-made, high-standing* quadruped which you have purchased : its price and your description lead me to expect a beast far preferable to poor Duncan.

As you read the *Scotsman* and *Courier* newspapers, intelligence of that plot[1] at London cannot but have reached you. It is a horrid piece of business—assassination has long been a stranger to the British soil : but whilst we deprecate such shocking attempts, some pity should be mingled with our abhorrence of the frantic conspirators. Well-founded complaints of poverty, one might almost say starvation, met with indifference or cold-blooded ridicule on the part of Governments, very naturally

---

[1] The famous Cato Street Conspiracy,—a plot for the assassination of the Ministers on the 23d of February, which, for a while, "absorbed every other topic of public interest."

exasperate the ignorant minds of the governed, and impel them to enterprises of a desperate nature. If the King and his ministers do not adopt a set of measures entirely different from those which they have followed hitherto, it is greatly to be dreaded that more formidable and better concerted resistance will ensue—or what is worse, that Britain, once the mistress of the ocean, and the renowned seat of arms and arts, will sink from her lofty elevation, her rude cliffs, no longer embellished by freedom, presenting only their native barrenness and in-significance. But I hope better of Old England yet. ·In the meantime, what constitutes *our*— wisest plan is to follow our private concerns as diligently as we may, without mingling in evil broils—unless imperious necessity call us so to do.

You are very just in supposing that the offer (poor indeed but the best the circum-stances will permit) which I made you was quite serious and unfeigned. I know not whether any channel opens in which you might try your commercial skill; but if it do, I would

certainly advise you to embrace the opportunity
—though it were but to instruct you with regard to what, I suppose, will be your future
occupation.   Command me, my boy, so far as
the few pounds I have are able to extend :
they will increase yet, I ween, by diligence and
activity.   I cannot employ them better.   But
lo! the end of my paper.   Excuse my dulness
—believe that I shall do better another time ;
and do not doubt that, I remain (my dear
Brother) ever yours most affectionately,

THOMAS CARLYLE.

L.—To Mr. R. MITCHELL, Ruthwell Manse.

EDINBURGH, 18*th March* 1820.

MY DEAR MITCHELL—Ever since the month—
of January last, a train of ill-health, with its
usual depression, aggravated by other priva-
tions and calamities too tedious to particularise,
has pressed heavily upon me.   The victim of
inquietude and despondency, I could not resolve
to afflict you with my sorrows or my dulness ;
and though conscience frequently accused me

of neglect, three months, you see, have passed away before the simple duty of answering your letter is performed. Though the period of my silence has been long, the excuse which I have offered might apply still longer; but my friends are too few, and my opportunities of acquiring more too slender for allowing me to stand such hazards : I cannot afford to lose the pleasure of our intimacy, and lest desuetude may cool (I trust it will not extinguish) that feeling, I write although it be "in spite of nature and my stars."

You would suspect me of a closeness, far enough from my disposition, if I did not attempt to trace you a sketch of the life which I have led for some time past. It must be a brief sketch for many reasons, however; and chiefly because it will contain no feature calcu- . lated to interest any one, even a second self. Zimmermann has written a book which he calls *The Pleasures of Solitude;* I would not have you to believe him : solitude in truth has few pleasures, uninterrupted solitude is full of pain. But solitude, or company more distressing, is not the worst ingredient of this condition. The thought that one's best days are hurrying darkly and uselessly away is yet more grievous. It is vain to deny it, my friend, I am altogether an unprofitable creature. Timid, yet not humble, weak, yet enthusiastic; nature and education have rendered me entirely unfit to force my way among the thick-skinned inhabitants of this planet. Law, I fear, must be renounced; it is a shapeless mass of absurdity and chicane, and the ten years, which a barrister commonly spends in painful idleness, before arriving at employment, is more than my physical or moral frame could endure. Teaching a school is but another word for sure and not very slow destruction : and as to compiling the wretched lives of Montesquieu, Montagu, Montaigne, etc., for Dr. Brewster—the remuneration will hardly sustain life. What then is to be done ? This situation—but I touch a string which generally yields a tedious sound to any but the operator. I know you are not indifferent to the matter, but I would not tire you with it. The fate of one man is a mighty small

concern in the grand whole of this best of all—
possible worlds; let us quit the subject, with
just one observation more, which I throw out
for your benefit should you ever come to need
such an advice.   It is to keep the profession
you have adopted, if it be at all tolerable.   A
young man who goes forth into the world to
seek his fortune with those lofty ideas of honour
and uprightness which a studious secluded life
naturally begets, will in ninety-nine cases out of
the hundred, if friends and other aids are
wanting, fall into the sere, the yellow leaf, and—
if he quit not his integrity, end a wretched
though ·happily a short career in misery and
failure.   Dissipation is infinitely worse : I thank
Heaven I am not a poet, I shall avoid that sad
alternative.

I was glad to learn that you had finished the
perusal of Homer.   Certainly the blind bard is—
little obliged by your opinion of him : I believe,
however, Candour is, and that is better.   If
from the admiration felt by Casaubon, Scaliger
and Co., and still more by the crowds that
blindly follow them, we could subtract that

portion which originated in the as hollow
admiration of others for the same object; and
if, further, all affectation could be banished; I
fear a very inconsiderable item would remain.
In fact Mæonides has had his day—at least the
better part of it; the noon was five and twenty
centuries ago; the twilight (for he set in 1453)
may last for another five and twenty centuries
—but it too must terminate.   Nothing that we
know of can last for ever.   The very mountains
are silently wasting away, and long before
eternity is done, Mont Blanc might cease to be
the pinnacle of Europe, and Chimborazo lie
under the Pacific.   Philosophy and literature
have a far shorter date.   Error, in the first,
succeeds to error, as wave to wave.   Plato
obscured the fame of Pythagoras, Cudworth
and Kant of Plato: the Stagirite and his idle
spawn have been swept away by Lord Bacon,
himself to be swept away in his turn.   Even in
the narrow dominion of truth the continuance
of renown is not more durable: each succeeding
observer from a higher vantage-ground com-
presses the labours of his forerunner; and as

the *Principia* of Newton is already swallowed up in the *Mécanique Céleste* of La Place, so likewise will it fare with this present Lord of the ascendant. Poetry, they tell us, escapes the general doom : but even without the aid of revolutions or deluges, it cannot always escape. The ideas about which it is conversant must differ in every different age and country. The Poetry of a Choctaw, I imagine, would turn chiefly on the pains of hunger, and the pleasures of catching Bears or scalping Chicasaws. In like manner, though some of the affections which Homer delineates are co-existent with the race, yet in the progress of refinement (or change) his mode of delineating them will appear trivial or disgusting—and the very twilight of his fame will have an end. Thus all things are dying, my friend,—only ourselves die faster. Man! if I had £200 a year, a beautiful little house in some laughing valley, three or four pure-spirited mortals who would love me and be loved again, together with a handsome library, and—a great genius, I would investigate the hallucinations that connect themselves

with such ideas.   At present I must revisit this
nether sphere. . . . . .

I know not whether I shall see you in
summer; most probably I shall leave this town
—if for ever I need not greatly care: but whether
or not, I need not add that I remain, my dear
Mitchell, yours ever,   THOMAS CARLYLE.

LI.—To ALEXANDER CARLYLE, Mainhill.

EDINBURGH, 29*th March* 1820.

Many thanks, my dear Alick, for your agreeable and entertaining Letter. . . .

You and my other affectionate friends at
Mainhill are very kind to press me so urgently
to come home.   I shall not forget this speedily.
The word home is sweet to a Scottish ear : and
I should be the most unthankful soul on earth,
if I did not gratefully reflect, that among all my
wants and disappointments, I have yet Parents
and brethren left with whom I can repose for a
season, and forget, in the midst of sincere affection, liberty, and vernal breezes, the smoke and

stir of this dull world. Of late I have often
been meditating to come home; last summer
was of very great importance to me, and had I
some stated job of work to keep me in employment and drive away "the vultures of the mind,"
I could spend the approaching months among
you with great advantage. I was happy at
Mainhill, happier upon the whole than I have
been in general since my boyhood; and though
we, degenerate posterity of Adam as we are,
have in our hearts a fund of *aloes* that would
chequer even the felicity of Eden, I hope to be
happy there again. Before writing, I expected
to have it in my power to give you some satisfactory account of the chance I have to get a
translation or other business of the like stamp
to manage in my rustication; and when the
box arrived, I was busy writing the lives of Sir
J. Moore and his father Dr. Moore, in order
that upon presenting them to Brewster to-
morrow, I might make some inquiries as to
this matter. What my success may be I shall
be better able to tell you next opportunity. In
the meantime I have some hope. I anticipate

· pleasure if I succeed;—rising early, evening *cracks*, Duncan's worthier representative (I mean the steed Duncan), and many things more, arise before the fancy: but if I should fail, as much doubt there is,—seeing "the best con- certed schemes of mice and men gang aft aglee," I shall not altogether droop. With health, I can turn me many ways; and I hope completely to recover that blessing. Dr. Brewster tells me that for fifteen years he was at death's door; and now in his forty-second year he is perfectly well.—After these lives above referred to, I have none to write, but those of Necker and Admiral Nelson, which will not be needed for six months. A review for Brewster's *Philosophical Journal* of a German book on Magnetism, I must also write or say I cannot; the former alternative is better: and then (as our man of law concludes in a few days) I am my own master, to go whithersoever I list. I shall make a violent effort to accom plish all these things:—and come home with a French or Latin book under my arm. Home any way.

I expect earnestly to see what are your opinions regarding Hume. Poor Carruthers! The strong and the weak alike wither at the touch of fate.—Write to me at large, and believe me to be, my dear Brother, yours most faithfully,

THOMAS CARLYLE.

LII.—To ALEXANDER CARLYLE, Mainhill.

EDINBURGH, 19*th April* 1820.

MY DEAR ALICK—I received your letter about noon; and being this day upon the fasting list (not from religious but medicinal motives), I have spirits to write but very imperfectly to you and not at all to my valuable correspondent Jack, whose letter, however, I esteem very highly on many accounts. In truth my silence is of small importance any way : I am coming home soon, and if once I "loose my tinkler jaw" among you, you shall get enough and to spare of it. This flitting plan is a most soul-tearing thing at best; and besides the unavoidable labour of packing goods and clearing scores, I have to strive with mul-

tiplied engagements relating to my summer's
employment. When I wrote last, I knew not
whether I should get any business at all to keep
my hands in use ; but it now appears that I am
to write several Articles for the *Encyclopædia* ⏤
(what they are I do not know—for I have just
been putting down a pretty long list, which Dr.
B. is to examine and select from and report
about on Friday morning) ; I have also two⏤
pretty long articles to translate which is the
easiest job; and lastly (which ought to have
been *first*) I have to write a kind of review of
that clear-backed large book which you will see
in the box—upon Magnetism and other points :
I ought to have done it here you know ; but I
felt my poor head so embarrassed and confused
with one thing and another that it seemed upon
the whole an easier plan to take the concern
home with me, and prepare it at my ease—
what ease at least I can find before the middle
of May, when it will be needed. I have likewise some (slender) hopes of getting a French
book to translate, *Life of Madame de Staël ;*
but of this I am far from certain, having only

Dr. Brewster for my henchman on this occasion, and he having no personal interest in the
affair. But whether his application, which he
was to make this day to one Tait a bookseller,
be successful or not, I shall have plenty to do
for one half-year : and though the money result-
ing from such labour is not at all abundant, it
is considerably better than the rewards of laziness. It will serve at least to keep the *Evil
One* out of one's pocket.

Now you will naturally be rather impatient
after all this preamble, to know *when* I am
actually to be at Mainhill. In brief then, my
project is this. I have promised to go and see
Irving at Glasgow before my return ; I design
to leave this smoky and most dusty town on
Saturday next ; the same night and next day
I shall likely spend with Nicol at Airdrie, and
on Monday I shall be with Ned. How long I
shall stay there is not so certain : it will depend
upon the state of the city, of Irving's engagements, etc. Upon the whole, however, it seems
likely that if all go well I shall see you about
Saturday (29th), or very soon after. It may be

before : but you are not to weary if it should be Tuesday or Wednesday, though I think *that* unlikely. I trust I shall find you all in good trim. . . . Yours most faithfully,

THOMAS CARLYLE.

The Radicals are quiet. How many lies have been told about them! Poor wretches! they are to be pitied as well as condemned. Cobbler Smith is in Edinburgh Castle.

LIII.—To Mr. JAMES JOHNSTONE, Annapolis, Nova Scotia.

MAINHILL, *5th May* 1820.

MY DEAR JOHNSTONE—It is vain to apologise or dissemble. I am one of the most careless, negligent, ungrateful dogs in existence. I ought without doubt to have answered your long-looked-for and most valuable letter by the very first opportunity. To have intended it, and gone directly to he Post-office for information about the Nova Scotia mails, is nothing : this long silence, the longest that has occurred in our correspondence, since we first had the happiness to know each other, gives you just ground to suspect that the lapse of a few months can obliterate all the traces of a long friendship from my mind, and render the duties of that honourable relation an empty name. I confess you have just grounds for such thoughts : and I despair of gaining credit when I assure you that in entertaining them you would do me anything but justice. Yet the fact is, I have not at any time forgotten you. Strolling about these moors last summer, the sight of Bogside,[1] of the sun setting in the *West*, and twenty other objects, incessantly and painfully recalled you to my memory : and in Edinburgh the presence of silly students with whom I could have no sympathy or fellowship recalled you still more painfully. Why then did I not write ? I know not ; I have said that there is no apology of a satisfactory kind, and I shall not attempt to offer you a frivolous one : but something like a palliation for my conduct may be found in the successive fits of

[1] Johnstone's home, near Mainhill.

activity and low spirits which occupied my time
last winter, in the paucity of our opportunities
to send letters to America, above all in the
desultory procrastinating habits which a fluctuating being like me is sure to contract, and
which steal away our minutes, we know not
how, till they amount to months or years of
time gone uselessly and irrecoverably by. It
seemed so easy when I had missed the January
mail (a few days after your letter reached me)
to be in readiness against the first Wednesday of
February; and when February and March had
both passed fruitlessly away the thing became
so painful to think upon, and Hill's projected
voyage to New Brunswick offered such a
flattering unction to my soul, that at last I
gladly resolved to postpone the operation till
his departure, which has been delayed several
weeks longer than was expected. I ought to
say also that I tried twice to write to you : but
the demons of dulness and disquietude shed
their poppies and their gall upon me ; twice I
attempted, and *bis patriæ cecidere manus.* Upon
the whole, I see well enough that I have made

out but a very lame case for myself; therefore
after all that I can say my only resource is to
throw myself on the mercy of the judge, and
to entreat him to hope that I shall never in
future behave so badly. If bulk can supply
other deficiencies you shall be satisfied; for I
design to scribble nearly all the paper in the
house.

I was going to congratulate you on the safe
termination of the voyage described so vividly
by your letter, and to express my hope that
time had already moulded your way of thinking
and living into some degree of toleration for
that of Annapolis; when I learned that your
new situation appeared likely to yield nothing
but discomfort and chagrin; that your boys are
stupid, your society brutish, your climate dis-
agreeable, and everything about the place
repulsive and disheartening. Alas! my dear
friend, I am grieved to the heart for it. That
by crossing the ocean you have not escaped
from care, is not surprising—she climbs the
deck along with us; she follows us to the
throne and the temple; the grave alone is

delivered from her visits : but that after so
much exertion, danger, and vexation you should
still find so little to sweeten the cup of life is
an affliction that I did not anticipate. Yet
what can I say to comfort you ? My words
cannot transform Acadia into Tempe, its rude
Planters into Roscoes, or its Trulliber into what⌐
a clergyman ought to be. Nor am I at all
prepared, even if I were qualified, to advise
you at such a juncture—the circumstances have
found me at second-hand ; I have been but two
days at Mainhill, and I have yet seen none of
your letters or correspondents. At first view,
however, it certainly strikes me that America
has presented its worst side to you. A new
situation commonly resembles a new suit of
clothes : rarely does it fail to gall the wearer
in some points at the beginning ; yet a little
while is generally sufficient to put all to rights,
to make the robe accommodate itself to the man
or the man to the robe. So may it fare with
your tutorship at Annapolis. I can easily conceive, for I have often felt, the forlorn sensation
that takes possession of the mind when no

object is at hand to interest it, and no other
mind to communicate with : I can understand
the painfulness of teaching, the trouble of interrupted habits, and twenty other inconveniences that your place abounds with : yet still
before determining (as I hear you have well-
nigh done) to revisit Europe, I would have
you steadily reflect upon the consequence of
such a step.   Can you determine to become a
schoolmaster finally, to perambulate the country
as a dissenting preacher, or to spend some
dozen painful years in the family of a paltry
squire with the hope of gaining an obscure
footing.in the Establishment.[1]   None of these
plans I think would suit you well ; yet they are
almost the only avenues which the literary pro-—
fession holds out for preferment to persons
in our station.   Even these poor avenues are —
in this country overcrowded ; one is jostled in
them at every step : other lines of life are not
less overcrowded ; and in place of times mending, it seems clear to most unprejudiced people
that the distress, not to say starvation which at

---

[1] The Established Kirk.

present involves the trading part of the com-
munity, must ultimately, and that ere long,
involve all the lower classes entirely. Nothing
then to be hoped but the dubious and distant
result of revolution and civil discord. This is
a pale and dreary prospect, my friend, which
Great Britain holds out to one; I fear, however,
it is too faithful. On the other hand, consider
how many of the evils that now torment you,
custom will inure you to endure with indifference, perhaps with satisfaction—consider the
pleasure of an independent maintenance—consider the boundless field which the new country
opens for exertion of every sort—a field not
impoverished like ours and disputed in daily
strife; but thinly occupied and fertile though
coarse. Consider all this, I entreat you, before
adopting a resolution which must now be final.
Fortune and the world conspire to chastise us
severely for inconstancy; and at our time of
life it is highly disadvantageous to change.

In all this long discussion, I have endeavoured to speak the cold and naked truth,
as it appears to my own mind, on considering

every circumstance that has come to my knowledge on the subject. I have endeavoured to
divest myself of every partial or selfish feeling;
because I consider that your demeanour on
this occasion may give a colour to the rest of
your life; and whoever takes upon him to
advise a friend ought to speak with an eye
to that friend's interest alone. It has cost me
an effort so to do in this case: few persons,
I suppose, have missed you more than I; and
though you, upon maturely contemplating both
sides of the question, determine to return to
Scotland, I shall be the very first to welcome
you with heart and hand to your native shore.
Perhaps you have views, which I know not of;
perhaps your agricultural skill might be exer-
cised in England more advantageously than
any of your other acquirements; I shall be
most happy to find it so: but I would not
advise you to lay any stress upon the pleasure
of spending another winter in Edinburgh; unless you have distinct prospects of putting the
knowledge you will acquire there to use, I
would not advise you to go thither even though

you were in Scotland and doing nothing.
Edinburgh looks beautiful in the imagination,
because the heart, when we knew it of old, was
as yet unwrung and ready to derive enjoyment
from whatever came before it.   Visit the *Alma
Mater* now, and you are disgusted, probably,
with the most feeble drivelling of the students
—shocked at the unphilosophic spirit of the
professors—dissatisfied with the smoke and the
odour and everything else in or about the city.
I certainly would not counsel you to make any
sacrifices, for what I know from sad experience
would almost without doubt disappoint you :
yet this, I think, ought hardly to weigh at all in
forming your determination.   Edinburgh may
have changed since we knew it—we ourselves
may have changed still more—yet after all,
there is a world even in Scotland, there is a
world elsewhere.   I repeat my request (and
with it conclude this prolix dissertation) that
you would steadfastly and seriously consider
the circumstances of the case—do nothing
rashly—and if you resolve to return back to
Annandale, be sure all your friends, and they

are not few, will experience the greatest satisfaction at beholding you once more.

After perusing the preceding pages, gratuitously consecrated to advice upon a subject which I know so imperfectly, you will be ready to infer that myself am placed on some commanding eminence, above the vicissitudes of Fortune, and qualified to cast down an experienced eye upon the vortex of human affairs. You were never in your life more mistaken. At no period, that I recollect, have matters had a more doubtful aspect. I went to Edinburgh in winter, after a summer pleasantly but not very profitably spent at my Father's, with the view of studying Scots Law—intending, as you know, if all things prospered to make one desperate effort at obtaining an Advocate's gown ; and gaining my bread by a profession recommended to my fancy so strongly by the honourable nature of the exertions that ensure success in it. I went in moderate health, and with considerable hopes: but alas! David Hume owns no spark of his uncle's genius ; his lectures on law are (still excepting Erskine's *Institutes*) the dullest piece of stuff I ever saw or heard of. Long-winded, dry details about points not of the slightest importance to any but an Attorney or Notary Public; observations upon the formalities of customs which ought to be instantly and for ever abolished; uncounted cases of blockhead A *versus* blockhead B, with what Stair thought upon them, what Bankton, what the poor *doubting* Dirleton; and then the nature of actions of—— *O infandum!* By degrees I got disheartened; the *science of law* seemed little calculated to yield a reward proportionate to the labour of acquiring it; I became remiss in my efforts to follow our Lecturer through the vast and thorny desert he was traversing; till at length I abandoned him altogether—with a resolution that if ever I became familiar with law, it must be under different guidance. Occasionally too I tried writing, but most of my projects in that department altogether failed. The silly Lives of Montesquieu, Montaigne, etc. etc., which I wrote for Brewster's *Encyclopædia* are not worth mentioning; the rest are yet in embyro. At length these incidents, aided

powerfully by the last horrible winter, began
to act upon my health : I determined to quit
Edinburgh ; and on Wednesday evening I returned once more to Mainhill—wearied and
faint, and though long used, not altogether reconciled to the rest which is enjoyed upon the
pillow of uncertainty. I am to translate and
write some trifles during Summer if my spirits
serve ; what next—— I am sorry that I care
so much more than I know. Upon the whole
I am altering very fast. Hope will not always
stay with one ; and despair is not an eligible
neighbour. I do not think I am ever to have
any settled way of doing. Teaching and
Preaching I have forsworn ; and I believe I
am too old for beginning any new profession.
One leads a strange miscellaneous life at that
rate : yet if it cannot be helped——

It must be owned, however, that I have no
great reason to complain. On looking at the
condition of many others there seems rather
cause for gratulation. Never in the history of
Britain did I read of such a situation. Black
inquietude, misery physical and moral, from

one end of the island to the other, Radical risings, and armed confederations of the higher classes, and little or no expectation of better times. This neighbourhood, I find, is suffering very slightly in comparison; on my way from Paisley I passed several groups journeying hither in search of work and food, like the Israelites of old to Goshen in the dearth : yet none can doubt that the Agriculture [*sic*] *must* feel the pressure of those taxes which at present exclude our commerce—except at a ruinous rate—from almost all the markets in the world. I am not a croaker ; but I forecast nothing except an increase of calamity for several years to come. I suppose you have heard fully from the Newspapers of the Radical commotions, the marching, countermarching, and battles that have marked this troubled winter. The disturbances are quelled for a season ; but as an old peasant, whom I overtook on the road from Muirkirk, expressed himself, unless these times alter, folks will all be Radicals together. One of the events which have occurred in the late troubles may affect you more than many other events of greater importance. I allude to the capture of William Smith, shoe-maker, Ecclefechan, who had travelled to Glasgow for the purpose of buying leather; and falling in with sundry men of kindred sentiments, had further invested himself with the character of delegate from our poor unpolitical village, and proceeded to act forthwith in that capacity. His dignity soon withered from his brow; and scarcely had he got his sentiments disclosed, when the room in the Gallowgate which those statesmen occupied was environed by a party of soldiers, and the whole fraternity of reformers, with poor Will among them, were lodged in Glasgow jail. Poor Sutor! I know not the extent of his criminality: but from the complexion of the times, I should not be at all surprised if he were sent to botanise in New Holland. I have much to say on the present state of public affairs; and if you were beside me, you would have to hear it all: but it is a little too much to occupy our brief interview with such matters—now that you are beyond the ocean and not at all concerned by them, and that I, though on this side of the great water, am so situated as to have nothing to hope and almost nothing to fear from any political change whatever. I consign you therefore if desirous of additional information, to two well-written Articles by Jeffrey in the last *Edinburgh Review*—and, if you know the maxim *audi alteram partem,* to sundry delirious speculations from the pen of Mr. Southey, wherein these points are handled at considerable length in the *Quarterly Review.*

I betake me to private history, in which, though with equal dulness and haste, I am sure of exciting deeper interest. . . .

And now, my friend, I must draw this wretched tissue to a close. My paper is coarse, my mind has been distracted and hurried by a thousand cross accidents since I began to write: I have written stupidly and tediously of course ; nothing has been as it should be but the wish to please you, which I do most conscientiously pretend to. I am persuaded you will pardon my inconsistencies and blunders for the sake of this last circumstance ; nay, further, that in spite

VOL. I.   X

of all my faults you will write me at immense
length by the ship's return. I have said that
it would not much surprise me if you returned
on board of her ; it will hardly please any one
so highly as myself : yet if so be not, if we must
not see each other for many long eventful years,
I hope both of us will always retain a happy
and heartfelt remembrance of the many days
we have spent together ; and neglect no opportunity of cultivating an intercourse so pleasant,
by every means that yet remains to us. My
Mother sends her most kind respects to you
and best wishes for your—safe return—so she
phrasès it ; my Father is prevented by absence
from joining at the present moment in this
wish, but Alick and Meg, who are beside me—
and every other heart about Mainhill—desire
to be most cordially included in it. Bogside, I
suppose, has written a letter by this conveyance
—so I have not mentioned any domestic news.
Edward Irving is at Glasgow, Dr. Chalmers'
Assistant ; I spent a week with him on my return from Edinburgh. He succeeds wonder-
fully. But I have room for nothing more.

Write to me as fully as you possibly can ; unless
you intend to bring *yourself :* and believe me
to be, with the warmest wishes for your prosperity, my dear friend, ever most faithfully
yours,
                                THOMAS CARLYLE.

LIV.—To JOHN A. CARLYLE, Academy, Annan.[1]

EDINBURGH, *7th December* 1820.

MY DEAR BROTHER JACK—I had no time last
night to write a reply to your lively little note ;
and besides, I gathered from some expressions in
it that you intended to write me by the Annan
carrier — Richardson as I conjectured ; — for
which reason I was the more willing to postpone the operation that so I might shoot two
dogs with one ball, *Anglice,* answer two letters
at once.   Richardson is here, and you have not
written ; nor considering the time, am I surprised at it.   You will write to me next time, I
know, at great length as to everything that

---

[1] John Carlyle was now at the Annan Academy, teaching
and preparing for College at Edinburgh.

concerns you. Be free in stating all your
doubts and queries and difficulties : I shall be
as free in answering them.

It is very fortunate that you have got Fergusson to hear you a lesson ; stick to it while
you have such an opportunity ; against winter
you will be ready for Edinburgh. I confess,
however, that I feel a reluctance in advising
you to diligence ; because I know you are likely
to be at least diligent *enough*, and present
appearances give me room to fear, not that you
will become a sluggard, but that you will become
a drudge—and thus being ever more enticed
by the charms of literature, and ever more re-
pulsed by the *foreignness* of everyday mortals,
that you will play the same miserable game that
I have played, sacrificing both health and peace
of mind to the vain shadows of ambition—un-
attainable by one of us, and useless though
they were attainable. Therefore, my good boy,
let me entreat you by the warmth of brotherly
affection—to beware of this, to guard against
the *first* advances of debility, to enjoy yourself
in society by every honest means, and to regard

it as a *certain fact* that continuous study will
waste away the very best constitution, the loss
of which is poorly, most poorly, recompensed
by all the learning and philosophy of the human
race. I fear you will not listen to me : young
men feel flattered when it is said they are studying themselves into ill-health ; but they bitterly
regret their conduct when it is too late. Believe my experience, my dear Jack ; may it
never become yours !

I have been led into these reflections, because
I am not yet quite recovered from a wicked
rebellion of the intestines—produced by the
change of air, I suppose, and also by inclement
circumstances in which that change was brought
about. I have studied none yet, and read next
to none. Indeed I must be re-established
before I *can* study to any purpose. . . .

I hope you still go home on Saturdays ; and
"janner[1]" for an hour or two with our dearly-
beloved Alick and other as dear friends. It
will lighten your spirits. Be good to my
Mother and Father—they have given us much,

---

[1] Janner, jawner = to talk idly.

the time is coming to repay it. But I must
out to walk, windy and dark though it be. Write
immensely to—Your affectionate brother,

THOMAS CARLYLE.

LV.—To ALEXANDER CARLYLE, Mainhill.

EDINBURGH, 2d *January* 1821.

MY DEAR ALICK— . . . I see easily that the
Black Dwarf and *Old Mortality* have hurried you
rather, in your epistle ; which, however, contains
the gratifying intelligence—still eminently gratifying, though happily it is common—of your
continued good health and peaceable situation.
The times are hard, my man ; and the hope
of their improvement is still distant : but with
a sound body and a free spirit, our life is not
without its charms. . . .

I am got better considerably, in point of
health ; so be not uneasy on that score. Health
I feel to be the greatest of all earthly goods—
the basis of them all ; and therefore I shall
study the maintenance of it with primary care.
I get low, very low in spirits, when the clay-

house is out of repair ; indeed I almost think at such times that health alone would make me happy; and in fact when strong outwardly, I seldom feel depressed within. . . . I have translated a portion of Schiller's *History of the Thirty Years' War* (it is all about Gustavus and the fellow-soldados of Dugald Dalgetty, your dearly-beloved friend); and sent it off, with a letter introduced by Tait the Review-bookseller, to Longmans and Co., London. Tait was to send it away very soon, in a package of newly published books, and to accompany it with a letter, setting forth that I was one of the most hopeful youths of the part, and that hence it were well for the men of Paternoster Row to secure my co-operation forthwith. The answer will come in (perhaps) three weeks. To say truth, my Brother, I am not sanguine in this matter : But now is not the time to discuss it, both because my paper is waning, and because out of fatigue from travelling I might give you too dark a picture of that and all my other schemes. . . .

Irving is a kind good fellow. He would

have me come and spend some months with him, because he thought I felt uncomfortable here; and he had all the *sappy* hospitality of Bailie Jarvie's children at command. William Graham[1] is also a friend and a deserving one : I could pass my time swimmingly among them : but I must work *with my own hands*, and work—while it is called to-day. You cannot conceive what a week I have had. Fat contented merchants—shovelling their beef over by the pound, and swilling their wine without measure, declaiming on politics and religion, joking and jeering and flowing and swaggering along with all their heart. I viewed them with a curious, often with a satisfied eye. But there is a time—for all. Last night, I was listening to music and the voice of song amid dandy clerks and sparkling females ; laughing at times even to soreness at the marvellous Dr. John Scott (see *Blackwood's Magazine*) ; and to-night, I am *alone* in this cold city—alone to cut my

[1] Merchant in Glasgow and Laird of Burnswark in Annandale ; of whom there is a long account in the *Reminiscences*, i. 164.

way into the heart of its benefices by the weapons of my own small quiver. Yet let us be of cheer, for *braw days are comin'* : and now, my boy, at this noisy season accept the prayer, put up for you and all our family, that many new years, and far happier ones, may be in store for each of us, that we may all love one another here, and in due time be made fit for that better land, where the just shall flourish, where the wickedness of men and the painfulness of Nature shall be hid from us, and peace and virtue substituted in their room!—Ever yours,

THOMAS CARLYLE.

LVI.—To ALEXANDER CARLYLE, Mainhill.

EDINBURGH, 10*th January* 1821.

MY DEAR BROTHER— . . . My possessions of worldly comfort are still mostly in *perspective*. Yet I live in hope, and no sooner is one scheme blasted than another springs up instead of it. Brewster is to settle with me about my *writings* whenever I like to go over : and what *might* be better he professes great readiness to furnish

me with a letter of introduction to Thomas
Campbell, who has lately been appointed Editor
of a Magazine in London, the publishers of
which are said to offer about fifteen guineas a
sheet. I *must* try somewhat for Campbell. O—
for one day of such vigorous health and such
elastic spirits as I have had of old! I will try,
however. Brewster came to me on the street
to-day, and talked long : he seems to feel that I
can be of some use to him, and *therefore* he
treats me gently. I was at dinner with him the
other day ; and *there* were Professor Wallis,
Telford the engineer, Jardine, another of the
same, ·and one Wright, a very ugly loud-
speaking man. They are persons to hear
whom would make one admire how they have
got the name and the emolument they enjoy
at present. Telford spoke of his "friend the
Duke" of this, and his "friend the Marquis" of
that—all honourable men. I left the party
without regret to sup with little Murray (you
recollect about him), where was to appear
McDiarmid of Dumfries and McCulloch, the
great McCulloch, better known to you as the

"Scotsman."[1] MᶜCulloch fell sick, and we had to content ourselves with one of his coadjutors —a broad-faced, jolly, speculating, muddle-headed person called Ritchie. I debated with Ritchie in a very desultory style about poetry and politics, less to his edification than surprise; and the dapper little MᶜDiarmid sat by as umpire of the strife. MᶜDiarmid is not "an elegant gentleman;" . . . in mental qualities he is estimable rather than otherwise—showy but unsubstantial—broad but shallow. . . .

After all, perhaps I shall fall into some agreeable society here, and finally be restored to something like steady peace and comfort. In the meantime, as you remark, I ought to be thankful that I am as I am. Witness Waugh! sad emblem of imprudence! Hunted by duns, destitute of cash, he has left his luggage to make good the payment of his lodging, and is now winding his zigzag way among the purse-bearers of Annandale, to raise a little money

---

[1] To become still better known as a writer on Political Economy, and the compiler of various useful works.

from the wrecks of his prosperity. No one but
pities Waugh, no one but blames him. . . .

[End of letter awanting.]

LVII.—To his MOTHER, Mainhill.

EDINBURGH, *Wednesday night*,
10*th January* 1821.

MY DEAR MOTHER— . . . I am afraid that
you take my case too deeply to heart. It is
true, I am toiling on the waves, and my vessel
looks but like a light canoe; yet surely the
harbour is before me, and in soberness when I
compare my tackle with that of others, I cannot
doubt hardly that I shall get within the pier at
last. Without figure, I am not a genius, but a
rather sharp youth, discontented and partly
mismanaged, ready to work at aught but teaching, and to be satisfied with the ordinary recompense of every honest son of Adam, food and
raiment and common respectability. Can I fail
to get them if I continue steadfast? No, I
cannot fail. The way, indeed, is weary; it leads
through a dry parched land wherein few waters

be; but how happy it is that I journey un-
attended by Remorse! that my conscience,
though it wound, does not sting me; that my
heart, when it faints, does not condemn! I
ought to be grateful that it is so; and to bear
these "light afflictions" calmly—they are not
sent without need.

You observe, Mother, I talk about my own
affairs most fluently: yet there are other affairs
about which I am anything rather than indifferent. It will be changing the direction
more than the nature of my thoughts (for this
also is one of *my* concerns) if I inquire particularly into your situation at Mainhill. *How*
are you? Tell me largely when you write. I
fear your health is feeble: I conjure you be
careful of it. Do you get tea—the weary tea—
alone now? By the little table *ben* the house?
I advise you to use it frequently: it is excellent
for weak stomachs. And do not, I entreat you,
let any considerations of thrift or such things
restrain you in those cases. None of us is rich;
but we should certainly be poor indeed, if
among us we could not muster enough for

such a purpose. Keep yourself from cold most carefully this unhealthy season, and read the *Worthies* or anything that will satisfy that high enthusiasm of your mind, which, however you may disbelieve it, is quite of a piece with my own. Do you still get the *Repository?* I observe there is to be a fresh Magazine at Glasgow, embracing the interests of the *United* Secession Church. I wish it could be got for you.

But here I must end. A happy new year to you, my dear Mother, and many, many of them —to be a blessing to us all! Write to me next time in the most ample manner. My best love to all the children.—Ever your affectionate son,   THOMAS CARLYLE.

Do you care about that fish? One kind costs 3½d., the other 2½d. per pound. Boil it, change the water, and—*beit*[1] butter.

---

[1] Scotch for " add."

X LVIII.—To JOHN A. CARLYLE, Annan.

EDINBURGH, 10*th February* 1821.

I send you the Virgil, my dear Jack, according to promise ; and I need not say how much
I wish you luck in the perusal of it. By help
of the notes, and marginal interpretation—especially if David still continues with you—I do
not expect that you will find much difficulty in
penetrating the meaning of this harmonious
singer : and though you are not likely to reckon
him "the Prince of Poets," you are still less
likely to miss being struck with the high elegance and regular flowing pomp both of his
thoughts and language.

I have a long sheet here before me, boy,
and the consciousness that I have lately written
you three or four most *leaden* letters, to inspire
me with greater eagerness for amendment : but
alas ! it is not to-day that I can amend. I have
not been in worse trim for writing this twelvemonth. If you saw me sitting here with my
lean and sallow visage, you would wonder how
those long bloodless bony fingers could be made

to move at all—even though the aching brain
were by miracle enabled to supply them with
materials in sufficient abundance. I have been
sick, very sick, since Monday last—indeed I
have scarcely been *one day* right, since I came
back to this accursed, stinking, reeky mass of
stones and lime and dung. . . . Were it by moral
suffering that one sunk—by oppression, love or
hatred, or the thousand ways of heartbreak—it
might be tolerable, there might at least be some
dignity in the fall ; but here !—I conjure thee,
Jack, to watch over thy health as the most
precious of earthly things. I believe at this
moment I would consent to become as ignorant
as a Choctaw—so I were as sound of body.

Upon the whole it seems very cruel in me
to describe my miseries in such glowing colours
(does it not ?) and make you unhappy, when all
that you can do for me is to *be* unhappy on my
account. The thing is so, I do admit, Jack,
but really I am grown a very weak creature of
late. The heart longs for some kind of sympathy : and in Edinburgh I find little of it—
except from the well-meant though ineffectual

kindness of Geo. Johnston, who indeed watches over me very attentively. Here was the *grit-stone* theologian, Crone, about half an hour ago —he had called upon me twice—not to ask for my welfare, but to glean information about a history of the West Indies, information which the dog means to utter as his own in some house where he is teaching. He said he was very sorry for me : I could have thrown him out at the window for his sorrow ; but contented myself with saying that I knew well how deeply my condition affected his most compassionate soul.

You need not tell any one of those things except Sandy—not our Mother or Father, it would but vex them ; and they are not young and strong and full of hope like you to stand vexation. Nor would I have you to trouble yourselves much on my account. I shall surely get over this yet : and if summer were come I am thinking it will be well to secure quarters about Kirkcaldy or some bathing town and transport myself thither with all my tackle, to enjoy the manifold benefits of such a station. There

is a project on foot about translating one
D'Aubuisson, a Frenchman's geology—a large
book, for the first edition of which I am to have
60 guineas—the same sum for every succeeding
edition. Brewster was *very* diligent in forward-
ing it; and though I neither like the book nor
the terms excessively, I feel much obliged to
him for his conduct. There is also an edition
of [*seal covers*] works with a Life about which
I [was] speaking to Tait—and [I have] not yet
been able to go and hear his answer, which,
however, I do not strongly expect to be favourable. Now with some such job as one of those
—with good sea-breezes, and decent people
about me, I think I could get quite whole and
well after all that's come and gone. This grievous state of languor and debility—the *only* thing
that can break my heart—I feel inclined to
hope may be but temporary, the transition from
youth to hardened manhood: in a year or two
it may be all gone. There is Waugh (*ey mon !*
etc.) was once ill, and now never knows the
name of distemper. Do not mind me, then,
my boy : be diligent at your studies—yet care-

ful of excess; and next winter you will live
with me here—and be my *comforter*, and I will
be your tutor in return. Give my warmest love
to all at Mainhill. Remember me to Ben
Nelson if you see him.—Your affectionate
brother,
                    THOMAS CARLYLE.

John Fergusson is come in, and I have con-
sented to crawl out with him and try the St.
Bernard's *spa*—a fountain on the north of
Edinburgh.

LIX.—To ALEXANDER CARLYLE, Mainhill.

KIRKCALDY, 19*th February* 1821.

. . . I know there is within me something
different from the vulgar herd of mortals; I
think it is something *superior;* and if once I
had overpassed those bogs and brakes and
quagmires, that lie between me and the free
arena, I shall make some fellows stand to the
right and left—or I mistake me greatly. . . .

I accompanied Irving over here on Saturday
last, took up my abode at the Provost Swan's,

and as on all hands they kindly invite me to
continue, I have allowed Irving to return, and
I am to continue here for a few days. ·

Already the sea-breezes are acting bene-
ficially on me ; and in two or three days I expect they will have set me in such a case that
zealous ·exercise will keep me moderately well
in *that* old smoky city—the smoke of which I
sicken at—even while viewing it across the
pure azure frith of Forth. You know this
"long town," and you can easily conceive with
what emotions of melancholy pleasure, of joy
and sadness, I traverse all the well-known turn-
ings of it. There is something mournful in the
view of a half-forgotten scene, associated with
many of our pains and pleasures, something
that reflects back on us the rapid never-ceasing
flight of time, and makes us solemn or pensive,
even though our recollections may be mostly of
sorrows that we are now escaped from. I view
Kirkcaldy like an old acquaintance that is fast
forgetting me, that I am fast forgetting : yet
there are some people in it whom I could wish
to remember and be remembered by. They

are not many ; they are the more valuable for
that. . . .

LX.—To his FATHER, Mainhill.

EDINBURGH, 25*th February* 1821.

MY DEAR FATHER—You would get the
letter addressed to Sandy from Kirkcaldy about
Thursday morning ; and I trust it would have
the effect of calming your solicitude on account
of my health and outward welfare, about which
I have lately given you so much unprofitable
anxiety.   The sea-breezes of Fife, and the kind
attentions of its inhabitants, produced the most
salutary results on me ; I grew better every
day, and in the course of a few weeks I doubt
not I should have been as strong as ever at any
period of my life.   It was with regret that I
quitted them on Friday to meet Irving here,
who, however, in the interim had been forced
to return home.   I felt in a state of decided
convalescence, which I am happy to add has
since continued without interruption.

　　.　　　.　　　.　　　.　　　.　　　.

At present I look forward to a busy and

therefore a contented summer, in which I shall accomplish much, and among other things the long-wished-for results of gaining for myself some permanent employment, so that I may no longer wander about the earth a moping hypochondriac, the soul eating up itself for want of something else to act upon, or a withered school-master eyeing my fellow-men with a suspicion and solitary shrinking, which should be peculiar to felons and other violators of the law.

In fact, matters have a more promising appearance with me at the present date than they have had for a long season. Besides Jack's letter and some others which awaited my return from Fife, there was one which I read with indifference, abandoning the proposed undertaking of translating D'Aubuisson (for which consult Sandy); and one, which I read with considerable interest, proffering to me on the part of Bookseller Tait to *become a candidate* for the translating of a French book, *Maltebrun's Geography*, which one Adam Black, Tait's brother-in-law, is engaged with at present, and designs to put into fresh hands. Two persons (unknown to me) are to submit specimens of their work, I am to do so likewise; and Tait assures me that, if Black had known sooner, there would have been no competition in the case. So that I am not without hope of getting this job, and if the judge be a correct one, of deserving it. You may think the latter proviso is like dropping feather-beds out of a window from which one is soon to be precipitated in person : but within my own mind, I feel a kind of assurance that I can surpass my fellow-translators, unless they are far superior to the usual run of such creatures. And if I divine right, it will be very advantageous for me : a steady employment (the book extends to five or six large volumes—of which only one and a part are finished) that I can address myself to in any humour—for it requires no study; and by means of which it would not be difficult to clear the matter of £200 per annum for a considerable time. I shall hear of it by and by—like enough I may fail in those expectations ; but we can do either way.

But my sheet is done and my feet are cold
—good reasons both for drawing to a close. I
long to hear news of you all ; but I suppose
Farries had stolen a march on you, or you expected me home. My love to all there.—Ever
your affectionate son,   THOMAS CARLYLE.

George Johnston and I have been working
all day at Maltebrun—or I would have written
to Jack and Sandy. They of course will write
at great length next opportunity.

LXI.—To JOHN A. CARLYLE, Annan.

EDINBURGH, *9th March* 1821.

MY DEAR JACK—I have wasted this whole
blessed evening in reading poetry and stuff,
while I should have been writing a substantial
life of Necker, out of materials accumulated
two days ago ; and now that eleven o'clock is
struck, I may as well devote the remaining
hour to your gratification, and my own, in
this new mode, which, if equally idle with
the mode it succeeds, has at least the merit

of amusing two at once. . . . I am considerably clearer than when I wrote to Sandy,
the day before yesterday, and I should have
been still more so had not this afternoon been
wet, and so prevented me from breathing the
air of Arthur's Seat, a mountain close beside us
where the atmosphere is pure as a diamond,
and the prospect grander than any you ever
saw. The blue, majestic, everlasting ocean,
with the Fife hills swelling gradually into the
Grampians behind it on the north ; rough crags
and rude precipices at our feet ("where not a
hillock rears its head unsung"), with Edinburgh
at their base, clustering proudly over her rugged
foundations, and covering with a vapoury mantle
the jagged, black, venerable masses of stone-
work, that stretch far and wide and show like a
city of fairyland. There's for you, man ! I saw
it all last evening—when the sun was going
down—and the moon's fine crescent (like a
pretty silver creature as it is) was riding quietly
above me. Such a sight does one good ;
though none be there to share it, except the
Jurisconsult—"poorest of the sons of earth."

But I am leading you astray after my
fantasies — when I should be inditing plain
prose. It is painful for me to learn that you
already begin to experience the effects of too
close application. Let it be a warning, my
dear Jack, I solemnly charge you ; or the issue
will make you repent it bitterly, when it cannot
be remedied. Why do you sit so constantly
poring over books ? Go out, I tell you; and
talk with *any* mortal to relieve your mind rather
than converse perpetually with the imagination.
What would you be at, man ? Your learning
is advanced most respectably; and depend upon
it there is a learning more available often than
the learning of books,—the learning of the ways
of men, which cannot be acquired except from
conversing with them and observing them.
Speak with all honest men then, enter into
their views, and be one of them. I have
suffered deeply from ignorance of this counsel,
which I offer you with all the warmth of fraternal
affection. Do not disregard it. I would advise
you also to bethink you of some Profession, on
which to fix your endeavours : for it is an un-

lucky thing to be drifting on the waves of chance as I am now, and must long be, without companion or guide on my track, which for aught I know may lead me into whirlpools or breakers after all. What think you of the Church? Or of Medicine? Or *can* you teach for a livelihood? Consider this matter, and write me about it fully. In fact you must study to be more copious in your details henceforth. Is not paper cheap, the postage nothing? And what need for caring *how* you write to *me*. Tell me everything—whether you are merry or sad—busy or idle—your whole *manière d'être et d'exister*. Is Waugh still with you? Remember me to the luckless. Are you teaching Ben? Is Davie teaching you? How do you like Maro? How are they at Mainhill? etc. etc. etc. . . .

But hark! the lugubrious chant of our watchman—"*ha-alf-pa-ast* twelve!" So Good-night, my boy. Go to Mainhill on Saturday, and say that my heart thanks them for all their kindness; and that if I do not get *quite* well in a week or two, I will profit by it. My love to

them all *nominatim.*—I remain, your affectionate
brother,   THOMAS CARLYLE.

LXII.—To Mr. R. MITCHELL, Ruthwell Manse.

EDINBURGH, 18*th March* 1821.

MY DEAR MITCHELL—I have just read over
your letter, and to show you that I am not
altogether extinguished in sloth, I sit down to
pen an answer instantly. The colossal Wallen-
stein with Thekla the angelical, and Max her
impetuous lofty-minded lover, are all gone to
rest; I have closed Schiller for a night; and
what can I do better than chat for one short
hour with my old, my earliest friend? I have
nothing to tell you, it is true; but the mere
neighbourhood of your image brings so many
pleasing though pensive recollections, so many
shadows of departed years along with it, that I
may well write *without* having anything to say.
And do not fear, my gentle brother, that I will
lead you into the mazes of Kantism; I know
you have but a limited relish for such mysteries,
and among my many faults, an enemy even would

not reckon the inordinate desire of making proselytes. As to Kant, and Schelling and Fichte and all those worthies, I confess myself but an esoteric after all; and whoever can imagine that Stewart and Hume, with Reid and Brown to help them, have sounded all the depths of our nature, or, which is better, can contrive to overlook those mysteries entirely,— is too fortunate a gentleman for me to inter- meddle with. Nor shall I trouble you with my views of men,—at least not greatly; and for a like reason. I have been a solitary dreamer all my days, wrapt up in dim imaginings, strange fantasies, and gleams of all things; so that when I give utterance to the sensations produced on me by the actual vulgar narrow stupid world of realities, you very justly think me on the verge of—*coma*. But toleration, man! toleration is all I ask, and what I am ready to give. Do you take your Lipsius, your Crombie, your Schweighäuser; and let me be doing with Lake poets, Mystics, or any trash I can fall in with: why should we not cast an eye of cheering, give a voice of welcome, to each

other as our paths become mutually visible,
though they are no longer one?

I meant to give you my history for the bygone months. It is easily done. I have had
the most miserable health—was in a low fever
for two weeks lately, meditating to come home,
and actually did elope to Fife; and during all
the winter I have had such delightful companions to interrupt my long solitudes, such
intellectual, high-spirited men as you have no
idea of. My progress has been proportionable.
It boots not, as you say, to indulge reproachful
afterthoughts. Indeed I have begun to apply
the all-consuming maxim *cui bono?* to study as
well as other things; and to ask how can it
serve one to be learned and refined and
elevate? Is it not to imbibe a feeling of pity
for the innocent dolts around one; and of disgust (alas!) at the thistles and furze upon which
they are faring sumptuously every day? The
most enviable thing, I often think, in all the
world, must be the soundest of the seven
sleepers : for he reposes deeply in his corner;
and to him the tragi-comedy of life is as pain-

less as it is paltry. But to return—I have tried about twenty plans this winter in the way of authorship; they have all failed; I have about twenty more to try: and *if* it does but please the Director of all things to continue the moderate share of health now restored to me, I will make the doors of human society fly open before me yet, notwithstanding my petards will not burst, or make only *noise* when they do: I must mix them better, plant them more judiciously; they *shall* burst and do execution too. But all this, you say, is nothing to the point—*what* are you doing? Teaching two Dandies Mathematics; who leave me (*Io Bacche !*) in a month; compiling for Encyclopædias (hewing of wood and drawing of water); I was translating—and am soon to Review. Waugh has relented, for his book is reeling like a drunken man,—got himself *re*-introduced to me, and sent over a book lately—Joanna Baillie's *Legends*, so I beg, Sir, you will view the embryo Aristarchus with all the gravity in your power.

But to retort the question, what are *you*

doing? Are such geniuses as we, think you, to live crammed up as it were in the stocks, pinfolded thus, and shut out from all the cheerful ways of men, for ever? And what are the levers you intend to use? Tell me seriously, and think of it seriously, for it demands consideration. I think your classical teaching plan bids fair if you mature it well; and really I would not advise any one to launch, as I was forced to do, upon the roaring deep, so long as he can stay ashore. For me, the surges and the storm are round my skiff; yet I must on— on, lest biscuit fail me ere I reach the trade-wind and sail with others.

This I confess is a very pragmatical *Frank-Dixon-ish* way of talking to you; but it is too late now for mending it. I shall be less figurative next time. . . . "My address" is in your hands; see how you will use it—diligently and soon, if you care a farthing for your old friend,

THOMAS CARLYLE.

LXIII.—To his MOTHER, Mainhill.

EDINBURGH, *Wednesday morning*
[March 1821].

MY DEAR MOTHER—Though you have not
said a word to me personally for a great while,
I am well aware that there is no one in the
world who has experienced more anxiety on
my account of late, or will experience more
satisfaction at being told that I am now
relieved from my state of languor and pain, into
a state of comparative strength and happiness.
I know not whether I am rightly thankful to
Providence for this great blessing, but certainly
I am "*unco gled*"[1] as your pauper said; and I
cannot resist the desire of communicating the
agreeable intelligence to you myself, though
very much straitened in time, and obliged, as
you see, to content myself with a half-sheet,
notwithstanding your well-known repugnance
to such penurious doings. Another object
which I have in view in writing to you is to
inquire most minutely into your own state of

---

[1] Greatly pleased.

health, which I fear is nothing so good as it should be. My dear Mother, let me counsel you to spare no trouble or care, with regard to this. Endeavour to avoid all things that will fret or discompose your mind, be as much as possible in the open air, and go about to visit your friends and acquaintance in the neighbourhood, whenever you can by any means go. I am most anxious to hear a full and *faithful* account of this matter from your own hand.

.   .   .   .   .   .

You must write to me, if you can find *any* time. I am ignorant, and not patiently ignorant, of all your movements. You must send me a description of the whole. For myself, besides what I have detailed in many recent letters to my various correspondents at Mainhill, there is little that I can add at present. I write a very little, read some and walk some; and that is almost all my history. Last Sabbath I was to hear Dr. M'Crie (Author of *Knox, His Life*), who preaches to [a] few poor people within two or three hundred yards of this. He is an earnest-looking, lean, acute-minded man ; with much learning and thought, but no eloquence. It did me good to see the poor people with their clean faces, their attentive looks, and to hear our own old *St. Paul's* and *St. Peter's* (venerable tunes!) chanted with so much alacrity and apparent devoutness. It brought the little meeting-house at home, and all the innocent joyance of childhood back, to mingle strangely with the agitations of after-life. But I have done. Is there any book that I can get you, or *any* thing that I can do for you? Speak if there is; and gratify your affectionate and thankful boy,

THOMAS CARLYLE.

LXIV.—To JOHN A. CARLYLE, Annan.

EDINBURGH, *Wednesday* [*March* 1821].

MY DEAR JACK—Twelve o'clock is past; but I confide in Garthwaite's unpunctuality a little, and send you two lines of advice about your studies merely—for about this time, I guess, you are reading the letter sent by Gavin, which will satisfy you on all other points.

You have certainly been very diligent if you

can at all read Virgil and Sallust in so short a
time. I really wonder at it. You must give
up the Georgics, however, I think, without
delay. They are the most uninteresting and
by far the most difficult of all Virgil's writings.
Take to the Eneid immediately ; you will like
it far better. Do you mind the Grammar?
and the scanning? Attend to *both* particularly.
For Sallust, you cannot go wrong. Catiline is
an admirable narrative ; and the writer of it
ever shows himself the same lynx-eyed, hard-
headed, bitter little *terrier ;* to whom nothing
was agreeable because nothing was pure ; and
still more because he was not pure himself.
Crispus was a *rip* of a body, in his youth.
When you read the Eneid do not fail to admire
the calm gracefulness, the stately and harmonious diction, the clear imagination of Maro ; but
do not [neglect] to have your *winnow-cloth*
expanded by the grandeur and immensity of
Milton, or your heart quickened by his stern
and elevated strength of soul. Each after his
kind. Think too that *you* (poor Jack in Bitty
Geel's) do actually read the very words and

admire the very thoughts that Augustus read and admired two thousand years ago, and all great men since. Let this be a spur in the head, which is better than two in the heel— than the pressure of want—that is—or the lucre of gain.

But do not, do not, I repeat it, neglect your morning and evening walks—and your talks and laughs and recreations. It is well to read Johnson's *Lives;* though the man is prejudiced to a pitch (see Milton and Gray), he has great power of head, and his insensibility to the higher beauties of poetry does not extend to the most complicated questions of reasoning. His Rambler is very good ; but not so amusing. Can you not get Shakespeare, or Byron ? Goldsmith's essays are "*capital*"—in style and liveliness. Dean Swift is a merry grinning dog. Did you ever see his *Tale of a Tub?* John Johnstone (Mrs. Dr.'s) has it and will lend it. Johnson's *Journey to the Western Isles* is likewise good. And *Don Quixote*—read it, till your sides crack, which they will do, if you have risi[ble or]gans. Try if you can get Russell's

History of Modern Europe. George Irving will procure it from the library of the burgh. Except the last, those things are principally for amusement ; yet if you attend to the style—and imitate it judiciously, they will profit you not a little. At any rate they fill the head pleasantly, and therefore usefully.

We shall talk of your school when I come home, about August or so. Perhaps you may get some teaching here, which will do better. Go on and prosper, my boy! There is no fear. Adieu!—Your affectionate brother,

THOMAS CARLYLE.

LXV.—To Mr. R. MITCHELL, Ruthwell Manse.

EDINBURGH, 4*th April* 1821.

MY DEAR MITCHELL—Your pupil George John having it in view to proceed shortly home again to Ruthwell, you cannot be surprised that I seize the opportunity which this circumstance affords me to disport a little in the way of innocent chat with you—and relieve my solitude by an *emblem* of society, since I cannot get the real article to my mind. *Le plus grand des—plaisirs, c'est l'abandon de soi-même :* in order to enjoy it, however imperfectly, I have kicked out the frolicksome Christopher North, and the " Monthly "—in spite of its paralytic affections, —with a host of other *écrivassiers*, who have beset me all day ; and confused me with their incessant and unmusical hubbub—driving all old thoughts away, and putting no new one in their room.

It is natural for you to expect that, seeing I have volunteered a letter, I must needs have some important news to tell you—something fresh in the literary world ; or at least something very strange in my own poor history. Neither of your suppositions is correct. The literary world is going on much as it was wont : frisking Reviewers come forth once a quarter, tipsy Magazinemen once a month ; both as usual

> " Trip it as they go,
> On the light fantastic toe,"

and see around them a nameless throng, digging like moles at Encyclopædias, Journals,

Monthly Reviews, etc. etc., quite in the old style. Nor has anything particular happened to myself since I wrote last to you. I am moving on, weary and heavy laden, with very fickle health, and many discomforts—still looking forward to the future (brave future!) for all the accommodations and enjoyments that render life an object of desire. *Then* shall I no longer play a candle-snuffer's part in the Great Drama; or if I do, my salary will be raised: *then* shall —— which you see is just "use and wont."

Our old acquaintances here are many of them alive; but few, very few of them, anything more. By "the long positive prescription" they have acquired a kind of right to live, and they exercise it quietly—travelling about the city to diffuse the knowledge of Ruddiman[1] and the *Horn Book*, consuming a stated, stinted portion of indifferent whisky punch, scenting every breeze for *dead* parsons, and trusting that Providence will not be blind to merit *always*. Such are the nascent pillars of our venerable

[1] Ruddiman's *Rudiments of the Latin Tongue* was for a century at least well known to every Scottish schoolboy.

Church.   I see few of them, and desire to see
still fewer.   Murray is here, with *his* Galloway
History.   Upon the whole, Murray is among
the best of them.   He has an inexhaustible
fund of activity—wishes greatly to be loved,
and takes the proper mode of becoming so : he
possesses indeed very little more than the small
peculium of knowledge customary in such
cases, but he has some warmth of heart, and
is not without gleams of a generous enthusiasm to cherish thoughts a little way exalted
above the mire and clay of mere physical
existence.   When Murray can snatch an hour
from his far-extended pedagogics, he visits me
now and then. . . .

They have got (*on a eu*) intelligence of
Frank Dixon.   He has eaten victuals with the
Governor of Bermudas, drunk kill-devil (rum-
toddy) with many of the planters there ; and
gives high promise of being useful in illuminat-
ing the heads and edifying the hearts both of
men and boys on that "ever-vexed" isle.[1]

---

[1] " Having no good prospect of Kirk promotion in Scotland,
he (Dixon) had accepted some offer to be Presbyterian chaplain

I hear not a word of poor James Johnstone. *Ubi terrarum*, where in all the world is he? If at New York still—he might have an introduction to a first-rate man there, did I but know his address. Poor James! I cry to think of the spoiler Time, how he dashes us unhappy worms far and wide,—now here, now there—in this noisy vortex of things. It is but few years since we three were—no matter.

My dear Mitchell, thou must write to me as soon as may be. Doubt not, I shall be more scientifical and philosophical and steady next time I reply. Really the fiend Mephistopheles catches one at times. Excuse his capers and his grins, believing that in spite of all, I remain in sincerity your faithful friend,

THOMAS CARLYLE.

My kindest, most respectful compliments to Mr. Duncan and his Lady.

and preacher to the Scotch in Bermuda, and lifted anchor thither with many regrets and good wishes from us all."— *Reminiscences*, i. 147.

LXVI.—To ALEXANDER CARLYLE, Mainhill.

EDINBURGH, 11th April 1821.

MY DEAR BROTHER—I had just concluded the first meal of the day now passing over me, when a tall wench interrupted my reflections, by lugging in that respectable box—the sight of which never fails to inspire me with agreeable ideas of various kinds. It gives me promise not only of substantial accommodations for the outward man, but also of intelligence refreshing for the inward man, and it holds out the prospect of an hour or two to be spent agreeably in transmitting intelligence from myself in return. The second gratification I have already enjoyed; the first is certainly in store for me ; and the last, you see, I am purposing to make sure of without delay.

Your sheet (the first real *sheet* for a long time) is well filled and pleasantly. . . , I daresay you are very busy at this period,—tilling the soil for potatoes, or harrowing it over corn, or *fallowing* it, or doing twenty things besides : so I do not look for such minute and comprehensive despatches yet as I shall get by and by. Only be as liberal as you can; do not fail to give me *something*, and I shall be satisfied.

There is nothing different in my condition, since I wrote last to you. . . .

We must all fight and fight—if we would live in this world. I often think they are happier that fight for solid necessary objects, than they that vex themselves in vain for dainty cates to satisfy the boundless cravings of a spirit left unoccupied. To see them hunting and drinking and debauching all ways; dancing, dressing, strutting—not to mention your great conquerors and projectors of various sorts— alas! the mind is languid and tempest-tossed and discontented, do what one will. Your husbandman keeps hold of Health any way; and I tell you the possession of that blessing is better than the empire of the world. If you could penetrate into the hearts of our poor shambling lairds—whether they be dandies or jolly ones, and see the yellowness and flatness of their inward landscape, you would fly with

double speed back to your fresh fields and brac-
ing air; gladly forsaking the switch and quizzer
and other *plaiks*[1] invented by French barbers
and the like, for the venerable plough—invented
by Father Adam himself, and dignified by the
usage of patriarchs and heroes, and still better
dignified intrinsically as the Upholder of the
human race.　But a truce with Philosophy.
There is no room for her here.

　Do you hear anything about Jamie Johnstone of late?　I have inquired often but without success.　Tell me next time: and *collect*
news for me from all parts, no matter how
empty.　I rejoice over the library, and its new
chance of existence.　Watch over it, in spite of
all opposition.　Write long, long: believing me
to be always, your faithful Brother,

THOMAS CARLYLE.

　What, in the name of wonder, is become
of Jack?

----

[1] Playthings, baubles.

LXVII.—To his MOTHER, Mainhill.

EDINBURGH, *Saturday* (*candle-lit*)
[*June?* 1821].

MY DEAR MOTHER—I have studied it and
find you must again be contented with a half-
sheet : my time is short, and my task is great
in proportion to it.   I read over your little
letter with such feelings as all your letters inspire in me, enlivened in the present case by
the assurance that your health is tolerable, and
your mind comfortable.   My dear Mother, I
trust Providence will long bountifully continue
those blessings to us—for it is to us more than
to yourself that they are valuable.

You need not doubt that I shall find employment for your generous anxiety to serve me :
indeed you can hardly require more employment, I think, than what you find in those lots
of clothes and stuff that I am ever sending
home to busy you with.   These are *bra'* white
socks, but really I needed them not.   And what
shall I say of the cakes ?   What but that I
have mumbled over fragments of them all the

afternoon? I suppose you put liberal allowances of butter in the dough—they are so much preferable, not to the last sample, but to the one before it. As for the butter, it is most welcome. . . . Many thanks also, my good Mother, for your bundle of camomile. I have laid it by in my trunk, and whether it help the stomach or not, it cannot fail to help the *heart* every time I look at it. . . . But alas! See how soon our little chit-chat is over—and I must take my leave. We shall meet in August. Pray that it be in peace and comfort. Goodnight, my dear Mother!—Your affectionate Son,

THOS. CARLYLE.

LXVIII.—To ALEXANDER CARLYLE, Mainhill.

EDINBURGH, *8th June* 1821.

MY DEAR ALICK—Your letter came most opportunely to relieve my anxieties on your account, and also to employ two hours of otherwise unprofitable time in answering it. . . .

I sighed to learn the fate of poor old Rose. She was a good beast in her day; but beasts

are mortal as well as men ; and like Cato's son,
our Rose "has done her duty." She has seen
you through the seed-time ;—which, if I may
judge from personal experience here, must have
been a task more than usually heavy. We
have had *such* weather ! Ever since May
began, a Whirlblast and a Drench, a Whirlblast and a Drench, have been our sad vicissitudes. Yesterday was a day of darkness ;
but it set the wind into the west, where I
solemnly pray it may continue as long as—
possible. Those easterly breezes with their
fine freights (of icy vapour, sand, straw, dung,
etc., here) are certainly the most entertaining
weather one can well fall in with. If you be
indigestive and nervous at the time,—it is quite
surprising. . . .

Irving was with me lately, during the General
Assembly time. The man could not have been
kinder to me, had he been a brother. He
would needs take me to East Lothian with him
for a day or two, to "see the world." We went
accordingly ; and though that wretched stomach
was full of gall—so that I could neither sleep

nor eat to perfection—I was happy as a lark in May. We returned last Thursday. I can say little about their husbandry—though I often thought had *you* been there what fine questions you would have put : but for the people—I saw the finest sample in the world. There was Gilbert Burns, brother of that immortal plough-man, "that walked in glory on the mountain-side, behind his team ;" there was—— But no sheet (much less *this*) can be enough for them. I came back so full of joy, that I have done nothing since but dream of it.[1] To-morrow I must up and study—for man lives not by dreaming *alone*. The poor paper you see is over with it. . . . Hoping that our Father and

[1] This was a memorable journey for Carlyle. He says of it in his *Reminiscences*, i. 174, " It was in one of these visits by Irving himself, without any company, that he took me out to Haddington [the county town of East Lothian, on the banks of the Tyne], to what has since been so momentous through all my subsequent life. We walked and talked,—a good sixteen miles, in the sunny summer afternoon. . . . The end of the journey, and what I saw there, will be memorable to me while life or thought endures," for then he saw Jane Welsh for the first time. " I was supremely dyspeptic and out of health those three or four days, and they were the beginning of a new life to me."

Mother and all the rest are well and happy, I remain as usual, my dear Alick, yours truly,

T. CARLYLE.

LXIX.—To Miss WELSH, Haddington.

EDINBURGH, 28*th June* 1821.

MY DEAR MADAM—It would have been a pleasant spectacle for. Mephistopheles or any of his sooty brethren,—in whose eyes, I understand, this restless life of ours appears like a regular Farce, only somewhat dull at times,— to have surveyed my feelings before opening your parcel the other night, and after opening it : to have seen with what hysterical speed I undid the gray cover ; how I turned over the poor tomes ; how I shook them, and searched them through and through ; and found—Miss Welsh's "compliments" to Mr. Car*slile*, a gentleman in whom it required no small sagacity to detect my own representative ! Upon the whole, I suppose, you did well to treat me so. I had dreamed and hoped, indeed ; but what right had *I* to hope, or even to wish ?

Those latter volumes of the *Allemagne* will
perplex you, I fear.   The third in particular is
very mysterious; now and then quite absurd.
Do not mind it much.   Noehden[1] is not come,
the London Smacks being. all becalmed.   I
hope it will arrive in time to let us begin
Lessing and Schiller and the rest, against
October, without impediment.   I shall send it
out instantly.

I had a hundred thousand things to tell
you; but *now* I may not mention one of them.
Those *compliments* have put the whole to flight
almost entirely : there remains little more than,
as it were, a melancholy echo of what has been,

Infantumve animae, flentes in limine primo.

Edward Irving and I go down to Annandale
about the first of August; he for two weeks, I
for as many months.   In the meantime, if there
is any other book that I can get you, or any
kind of service within the very utmost circle of
my ability, that can promote your satisfaction

[1] Noehden's *German Grammar*, which Carlyle had ordered
from London for Miss Welsh.

even in the slenderest degree,—I do entreat
you earnestly to let me know. This is not
mere *palabra;* it originates in a *wish* to serve
you—which must remain ungratified, I presume,
but is not the less heartfelt on that account.
Farewell!—I am always, your affectionate
friend,
                                    THOMAS CARLYLE.

Irving's packet was duly forwarded.

LXX.—To JOHN A. CARLYLE, Annan.

EDINBURGH, 19*th July* 1821.

MY DEAR JACK— . . . I do not precisely
know what week I shall be down ; but it cannot
easily be beyond the third or so from this date.
. . . I am going to *ride* continually when I
get home ; it is better than walking : and often
as I have been baulked, I am not without hope
of finding permanent benefit from the operation. At all events I must try : without some
improvement in the constitution, I am as good
as dead in the eye of law already ; good for
nothing but lolling about the room, reading

poetry, imagining and fancying and fretting and
fuming—all to no purpose earthly. I have
studied none or written none for many days.
Nevertheless I am moderately comfortable or
even happy at present. My confidence in
Fortune seems to increase as her offers to me
diminish. I have very seldom been poorer
than I am, or more feeble or more solitary (if
kindred minds form society); and yet I have
at no time felt less disposition to knuckle to
low persons, or to abate in any way of the stubborn purposes I have formed, or to swerve from
the track—thorny and desolate as it is—which
I have chosen for journeying through this
world. I foresee much trouble before me, but
there are joys too: and, joy or not joy, I must
forward now. When you launch a boat upon
the falls of Niagara, it must go *down* the roaring
cataract, though rocks and ruin lie within the
profound abyss below: and just so if a man
taste the magic cup of literature, he must drink
of it for ever, though bitter ingredients enough
be mixed with the liquor. . . .

Do not too proudly look down upon the

society you can find in Annan. Believe my
sad experience, *that* is a sad error. I know
well enough your comrades are "a feeble folk ;"
but still they are *a* folk ; and depend upon it,
you will repent this gloomy seclusion of yourself
from their accustomed haunts—how barren and
beaten soever—if you persist in it. There is
no real happiness, Jack, out of the common
routines of life. Happy he who can walk in
them daily, and yet ever be casting his eye over
the sublime scenery which solicits us from the
far and elevated regions of philosophy ! I have
missed this rare combination, you observe, and
I am paying for it. Do not you do likewise !
Be social and frank and friendly with all honest
persons. Practice will soon make it easy, and
the reward is wholesome and abundant. Go
out, I bid you, from the *camera obscura* of *Bitty
Geel;* go out frequently and talk—talk even
with the Jurist, Fergusson, Irving, or any of
them.

When I get home, I am going to exhibit all
this more at large and in more luminous order
—appealing to myself, as I may well do, for

proof experimental of a theory which I can so easily demonstrate *à priori.* Muster all your counter-arguments before my appearance. And *when* will that be ? So soon as I have got that beggarly article *The Netherlands* (for which I can find next to no materials) off my hands,—and I began working at it some days since. Irving and I spoke of travelling by the west somewhere : we have not arranged it yet. But this Netherlands is the main bar ; I have no *pluck* in me for such things at present—yet it must be *clampered* together in some shape, and shall if I keep wagging. Tell David Fergusson that I am charmed with his manuscript ; it is the prettiest ever was written for the *Encyclopædia,* and perfectly correct. I shall give you enough to write in harvest—at present I have nothing.

.   .   .   .   .   .

My love to all at Mainhill, including Nancy, our cousin, if she be with you still. Adieu !— Your affectionate Brother,

THOMAS CARLYLE.

LXXI.—To his MOTHER, Mainhill.

EDINBURGH, *Saturday evening*
[*July* 1821].

MY DEAR MOTHER—I have still a few
minutes on hand before the time of delivering
up my packet to the care of Garthwaite; I
cannot easily employ them better than in writing a line or two for your perusal. A line or
two, you see, is all that this paper will hold;
and in fact I do not need much more. I am
to see you very soon, when we shall meet over
a savoury dish of tea *down-the-house;* and discuss in concert all that has happened to each
of us since we parted. That will be a much
finer method than the tardy plan of exchanging
letters—which, however copious, are always a
very unfaithful and inadequate emblem of the
truth.

I care not how soon I were down at Mainhill: for this city is fast getting very unpleasant. The smell of it, or rather the
hundred thousand smells are altogether pesti-
lential at certain hours. And then the dust,

and, more than all together, the *noise*—of many
animals, and many carts, and fishwives innumerable; not to mention the men selling
water (of which there is a thirst and a scarcity
here), armed with long battered tin-horns, that
utter forth a voice, to which the combined
music of an ass, a hog, and fifty magpies all
blended into one rich melody were but a fool.
The man wakens me every morning about
seven of the clock, with a full-flowing screech,
that often makes me almost tremble.

I hope you are getting into better health
now when the weather is bright and invigorat-
ing. Have you ever got down to sea-bathing
this summer? You should try it *by all means.*
It is quite a specific to me; if I lived by the
shore, I am almost certain I should recover
completely. This last winter and spring I
have had more light thrown upon your various
indispositions than I ever got before. I may
say I never till lately knew how to pity you as
I ought. These nerves when they get deranged are the most terrific thing imaginable.
I do entreat you, my dear Mother, to take the

most minute and scrupulous charge of your health—for the sake of us all. No one can tell what you have endured already—take care! take care! As to news or anything of that sort, you will find all I have to say in the boys' letters. At any rate you see, the paper is finished, and I must withdraw. Give my love to my Father and all the *wee things*—not forgetting Nancy if she is still with you.—I am always (my dear Mother) your affectionate Son,

THOS. CARLYLE.

LXXII.—To ALEXANDER CARLYLE, Mainhill.

EDINBURGH, *9th August* 1821.

MY DEAR ALICK—I have merely a few minutes to write you in ; and my head is turn-ing sadly during the operation—for I have been dining and *gaffaaing* with one Nichol, a Mathematical Teacher here. But half a minute would suffice to say all my say ; which is only to tell you that I design to come home forth-with, that is to say, on Monday next, the 13th

of August, in the year of Grace eighteen hundred and twenty-one.   I shall mount the Dumfries mail-coach about eight of the clock on
that important morning : and I expect to be
in Moffat (no miracle occurring to stop me)
about four in the afternoon.

Therefore, my dear Alick, you will proceed
instantly, on receipt of this, and attach the
quadruped Dumple to the rack, giving him
what corn and hay he is able to consume ;
that so on Monday morning that famous
charger may be strengthened to undertake the
journey to Moffat, and transport my carcass
down to Mainhill upon his back. . . .

Within the last three weeks, I have written
almost as much as I had ever written before in
the whole course of my natural life.   Not only
my own two stipulated Articles, but *another,*
which the very shifty Editor called upon me
not to write only but to *manufacture*, the proper
Author, one Erskine, a Laird, having fallen
sick,—or gone stupid (I should say *stupider*),
and not being able to finish what he had already begun and even got printed.   It was

such a job. But I have done it all now ; and spite of that wretched *bog*, I am merry as a maltman. They are printing it even now ; and *if* you but saw my table ; how it is covered with manuscripts and first copies and proof-sheets and pens and snuffers and tumblers of water and pipes of tobacco ! But no matter.

On Monday morning then, you will start about nine o'clock and meet me pointedly. If *you* cannot come, even Jamie would do ; but you would do better. Should circumstances prevent you, however, do not mind it : I shall wait till eleven, and then ascend the Glasgow mail—appearing, in that case, at Mainhill before duck-rising.

. . . I was going to bid you call for *this* letter on Saturday ; but I am a Scot and no Irishman to produce *bulls;* therefore I trust to Fate that you will get the news on Sunday at farthest.

Good-night, my dear Alick ! I am amazingly sleepy—but notwithstanding always, your affectionate Brother,   THOMAS CARLYLE.

LXXIII.—To Miss WELSH, Haddington.

MAINHILL, ECCLEFECHAN,
1st September 1821.

MY DEAR MADAM—On again noticing this crabbed hand of mine, I fear you are ready to exclaim with some feelings of surprise and displeasure : Why troublest thou me ? To this very natural question it were tedious and difficult to make any satisfactory reply. The causes which give motion to my pen at present are too vague and complicated for being discussed in the preface to a single letter; and hardly of importance enough to a second person for being discussed anywhere. Perhaps it is more expedient, as it is certainly easier, to throw myself on your good-nature at once; to supplicate your indulgence if I prove tiresome, your forgiveness if I be so unfortunate as to offend. You know well enough it is far from my intention to do either : and cases are every day arising in which a generous person finds it just to let the innocence of the purpose serve as an excuse for the faultiness of the deed.

Upon this principle, if on no other, I entreat
you, *be not* angry with me! If you saw into
my views properly, I am sure you would not.

The truth is, in this remote district, where
so few sensible objects occur to arrest my
attention—while I am too sick and indolent to
search for intellectual objects—the Imagination
is the busiest faculty, and shadows of the past
and the future are nearly all I have to occupy
myself with.   But in the multitude of anticipations and remembrances, it is quite conceivable
that your image should be occasionally present
with me : and all men love to talk or at least to
write on subjects about which they often think.
Nor is it merely as an absent friend that I
contemplate you, and have a kind of claim to
converse with you.   It is impossible for me,
without many *peculiar* emotions, to behold a
being like you entering so devotedly upon the
path of Letters, which I myself have found to
be as full of danger as it is of beauty : and
though my own progress in it bears but indifferent testimony to my qualifications as a
Guide, I may be allowed to offer you the result

of my experience, such as it is, and to pronounce the "Good-speed!" which I wish you
in silence so frequently and so cordially.

I am not now going to depreciate your
studies, or tease you with advices to abandon
them. I said enough on that side of the question when we were together last; and stupidly
—as native dulness, exaggerated by a sleepless
week, and the fat contented presence of Mr.
B. could make me say it : and after all I
believe my habitual opinion is not of that sort.
To me those pursuits have been the source of
much disquiet; but also of some enviable enjoyment : if they have added a darker shade to the
gloom of my obscure destiny, I ought not to
forget that here and there they have chequered
it with a ray of heavenly brightness, which
seemed to make amends for all. The case is
similar with every one that follows literature :
it increases our sensibility to pleasure as well as
pain ; it enlarges the circle of objects capable of
affecting us; and thus at once deepens and
diversifies the happiness and the misery of our
life. The latter in a higher ratio, I fear : yet

here it is often blamed unjustly ; there are per-
turbed souls to whose unrest it gives direction
rather than existence : and though the charge
were altogether just, what could be made of it ?
Happiness is not our final aim in this world—
or poor Shandy [1] would be the finest character in
the nation.   It is the complete development of
our faculties—the increase in capacity as sen-
tient and thinking creatures, that constitutes the
first want : and as mental excellence—to think
well and feel nobly—is doubtless the highest of
all attainments—so the mental nourishment
which literature affords, as richly as any object
of human activity, should stand among the
foremost of our desires.   Nourishment of any
kind may, indeed, by injudicious application, be
converted into poison ; and mental nourishment
forms no exception to the rule.   But if its *abuse*
may lead to isolation from our brethren, and to
every species of wretchedness, its prudent *use*
does not of necessity exclude from any other

---

[1] Miss Welsh's dog.   See Carlyle's *Miscellanies* (Library
Edition, v., 267, *n.*) for this Shandy's interviews with Sir
Walter Scott !

source of happiness. Often, it is true, the studious man wanders in solitude over rocky and tempestuous regions ; but sometimes a lovely scene will strike his eye as well as that of another, and touch him more keenly than it does another :—some sweet sequestered dale, embosomed calmly among the barren mountains of life,—so verdant and smiling and balmy —so like a home and resting-place for the wearied spirit, that even the sight of it is happiness : to *reach* it would be too much ; would bring Eden back again into the world, and make Death to be indeed, what cowards have named him, the enemy of man. Oh that it lay with me to show you the means of securing all the benefits to be found in such pursuits, without any of the harm ! But it may *not* be. The law of our existence is that good and evil are inseparable always : the heart that can taste of rapture must taste of torment also, and find the elements of both in all things it engages with. Nevertheless I counsel you to persevere. In your advantages natural and accidental, there exist the materials of a glorious life : and if in cultivating the gifts of your mind, you can but observe the *Golden mean*, which it is so easy to talk of, so difficult to find—if in striving after what is great and productive of honour, you do not *too* widely deviate from what is common and productive of comfort—the result will not still be unmixed, but I shall join with thousands in rejoicing at it. The hazard is great, the alternative appalling ; but I augur *well*.

My sheet is done while my subject is scarce begun. Shall I not have another opportunity to enter on it ? I still entertain a *firm trust* that you are to read Schiller and Goethe with me in October. I never yet met with any to relish their beauties ; and sympathy is the very soul of life. This letter is amazingly stupid. It is enough if it recall to your memory, without displeasure, one who desires your welfare in every sense as honestly as he can desire anything.—Your sincere friend,

THOMAS CARLYLE.

LXXIV.—To Mr. R. MITCHELL (care of
Mr. T. Murray, Edinburgh).

MAINHILL, 3*d October* 1821.

MY DEAR MITCHELL—I was down at Ruthwell the other week, and got the two books
which you so punctually left for me ; but as the
promise recorded on the slip of paper stuck into
Keill[1] seems likely to be rather tardy in its
fulfilment, I am going to interrupt your repose
with a reason unconnected with borrowing or
lending.   I owe you an apology for my un-
ceremonious desertion of our appointment : but
I suppose you have already excused me.
Murray will have told you the cause of
my failure ; how I went into Galloway, and
rode and ran in all directions there without
measure.   How could I withstand such an
opportunity of gadding ?   You cannot but
forgive me.

In our perambulations through "that Attica
of Scotland," the Historian and I did not fail

---

[1] Probably *Introductio ad veram Physicam*. See Letter XII.,
supra.

to revisit the intended scene of your didactic
labours, and to muse a little on the fruits which
the Tree of Knowledge, pruned and watered
by your steady hand, is likely to produce to
yourself and the youth of Kirkcudbright.   Our
augury was favourable : and I rejoiced in-
dividually in the thought that my oldest,
nearly my only, College friend had found so
fair an arena for exhibiting his talents in the
way most agreeable to himself, and acquiring
some portion of those rewards which honest
industry has the best of all rights to claim.
Of the Gallovidian Capital I know nothing in
particular : but I can easily predict that in com-
mencing your functions, and even in proceeding
with them regularly, you will have much to
strive with, which your previous experience
has made you but imperfectly aware of.
Human nature is nearly the same every-
where : and the tie by which a schoolmaster
is connected with his employers is at all times
of so galling a kind, that there is no wonder
both parties should wince under it occasionally.
Busy-bodies will be forward to offer you

advices, remonstrances, complaints; the completion of your ideal schemes will be marred in part (it is but the continual destiny of man!) by the ungainliness of your materials; and at first, it is likely, you may languish under the want of congenial society, and *such* a home as you enjoyed at Ruthwell. My own experience of these things is trifling and unfavourable; yet I do not reckon the problem of succeeding in a school, and learning to remedy or endure all its grievances, one of extreme difficulty. First, as in every undertaking, it is necessary, of course, that you *wish* to succeed; that you determine firmly to let nothing break your equanimity, that you "lay aside every weight" —your philosophical projects, your shyness of manner (if you are cursed with that quality), your jealous sense of independence—everything in short that circumstances may point out as detrimental to your interest with the people; and then, being thus balanced and set in motion, your sole after duty is to "run with patience:" you will reach the goal undoubtedly. Public favour in some sense is requisite for all

men ; but a Teacher ought constantly to bear
in mind, that it is life and breath to *him :*
hence in comparison with it nothing should be
dear to him ; he must be meek and kindly and
soft of speech to every one, how absurd and
offensive soever.   To the same object he must
also frequently sacrifice the real progress of his
pupils, if it cannot be gained without affecting
their peace of mind.   The advantages of great
learning are so vague and distant, the miseries
of constant whining are so immediate and mani-
fest, that not one parent in a thousand can take
the former in exchange for the latter—with
patience—not to speak of thankfulness.   For
the same reason he must (if the fashion of the
place require it) go about and visit his employers ; he must cook them and court them by
every innocent mode which the ever-varying
posture of circumstances will suggest to a mind
on the outlook for them.   This seems poor
philosophy—but it is true.   The most diligent
fidelity in discharging your duties will not serve
you—by itself.   Never forget this—it is mathe-
matically certain.   If men were angels, or even

purely intellectual beings having judgment and no vanity or other passion, it might be different; but as it is, the case becomes much more complicated—few, very few, had not rather be cheated than despised, and even in the common walks of life, probity is often left to rot without so much as being praised. It has the *alget* without the *laudatur;*[1]—which is a most sorry business doubtless.

I have written down all this, my dear Mitchell, not because I thought you *wanted* it; on the contrary, I imagine your talents and manners and temper promise you a distinguished success; but because I thought the fruit of my painful experience might be worth *something* to you, and that something, however small, I was anxious to offer you. Take it, and call it the *widow's mite*, if you like. It is from your friend,   T. CARLYLE.

Will you let me know where you are, and

---

[1] —— " probitas laudatur et alget."
JUVENAL, *Sat.* i. 74.

when you intend coming Southward? I must see you before you move westward: I know not when I shall go to Edinburgh. Its reek— and stench are hateful to me.

END OF VOL. I.

Printed by R. & R. CLARK, *Edinburgh.*

.

www.ingramcontent.com/pod-product-compliance
Lightning Source LLC
Chambersburg PA
CBHW030901270326
41929CB00008B/517

Thomas Carlyle, Charles Eliot Norton

Early Letters
Edited by Charles Eliot Norton. Vol. I (1814 - 1821)

ISBN/EAN: 9783744688475

Printed in Europe, USA, Canada, Australia, Japan

Cover: Foto ©Thomas Meinert / pixelio.de

More available books at **www.hansebooks.com**

EARLY LETTERS

. OF

THOMAS CARLYLE,

EDITED BY

CHARLES ELIOT NORTON

VOL. I.

1814—1821

𝔏𝔬𝔫𝔡𝔬𝔫

MACMILLAN AND CO.

AND NEW YORK

1886 .

ERRATA

PREFACE

Mr. Carlyle was for many years, especially during his early manhood, an industrious letter-writer. A great many of his letters have been preserved and are in the possession of his niece, Mrs. Alexander Carlyle. It is at her desire that I have undertaken to edit a selection of them.

"Express biography of me I had really rather that there should be none," said Carlyle in his Will, and a biography of him, correct at least if meagre, might perhaps have been gathered from his letters, his *Reminiscences*,[1] and the *Memorials of Jane Welsh Carlyle*.[2]

---

[1] *Reminiscences, etc.*, edited by J. A. Froude, 2 vols. London, 1881.

[2] *Letters and Memorials of Jane Welsh Carlyle.* London, 1883.